A CONCISE HISTORY OF

Germany

CONSTANTINE FITZGIBBON

with 191 illustrations

THAMES AND HUDSON · LONDON

*To Margot Pottlitzer
with affection and with thanks*

Frontispiece: Berlin. An East German guard patrolling
the Wall, with the Brandenburg Gate in the background.

Picture research: Alla Weaver

© 1972 Thames and Hudson Limited, London

Printed in Great Britain by Jarrold and Sons Limited, Norwich

ISBN 0 500 45013 7

F,

FITZGIBBON

A Concise History of Germany

943

FIT

This book is due for return on or before the last date
shown above but it may be renewed unless required
by other readers, by personal application, post, or
telephone, quoting this date and the author and title.

BUCKINGHAMSHIRE COUNTY LIBRARY

L28

A CONCISE HISTORY OF Germany

CONTENTS

CHAPTER ONE

What is Germany?

From 1815 at the latest to 1848 Prince Metternich, the Austrian chancellor, was one of the most astute and perhaps the most powerful political figure in continental Europe. Italy was then aspiring to nationhood. Metternich, whose Austria controlled part of the neighbouring country, would have none of this. Italy, he said and we can almost hear the sneer in his voice, is 'a geographical expression'. Two generations earlier, when Metternich's Austria still styled itself the Holy Roman Empire, Voltaire had remarked that it was neither holy, nor Roman, nor an empire. In theory the emperor, from Vienna, claimed sovereignty over the multitude of German states, kingdoms and principalities, and had done so since the crowning of Charlemagne in the year 800, who had of course set far wider boundaries to his empire than this. In theory, too, the imperial throne was electoral,

Charlemagne with his son, King Pepin of Italy. Tenth-century copy of ninth-century MS (*above*).

Charles IV and the seven Electors, *c.* 1370.

the electors being the rulers of the more important component states, nor need the emperor even be a German. In fact from the Middle Ages the Habsburg dynasty pre-empted the imperial power, and from the time of the Reformation the reality of that power steadily diminished in what is now Germany, though extended eastwards into Hungary, Bohemia, southern Poland, the Balkans, and was maintained in northern Italy. In the last few centuries of its life, before its dissolution in 1815 and its replacement by the Austro-Hungarian Empire (1815–1918), it was, like its successor state, an international organism. It was never a German empire in any meaningful political sense, though German and Latin were its principal administrative languages. What, then, are we to make of Germany? Before describing its history, it would be as well to define the country under discussion. This, however, is easier said than done.

A geographical expression? Germany was frequently, and correctly, referred to as 'the Germanies' until Bismarck's creation of a nation-state in 1871, enlarged by Hitler in 1938, 1939 and 1940 to include almost all the German-speaking peoples of Europe (except German-speaking Jews) within his short-lived Greater German Reich, and promptly fragmented again into three by the victorious Allies in 1945: Austria, the state that was to be called the German Federal Republic, and the Soviet colony that calls itself the German Democratic Republic. The German-speaking people of Alsace became once again Frenchmen by law, the South Tyrolese remained Italians, and those few who were not driven out of the Eastern European states reverted to their pre-war nationalities. The pompous but beautiful (Haydn wrote the music, Hoffmann von Fallersleben the words) German national anthem makes a rough and inaccurate guess at Germany's territorial boundaries. From the Etsch, it says, to the Belt. The Belt is two sea passages north of Denmark (the word is the same as Baltic) and has never been any sort of a German frontier. The Etsch (Italian 'Adige') is a Tyrolean river that flows into the Adriatic. Once upon a time, in the Middle Ages, it was for a while the frontier of the Holy Roman Empire, but was never a German frontier. The western frontier of Germany, or the Germanies, has been the cause of a long series of wars between the Germans and the French, who have at times claimed that their 'natural' frontier is the Rhine. 'Nous l'avons eu, votre Rhin', Alfred de Musset wrote, quite correctly but ominously, after Napoleon's imperialist dreams had finally collapsed at Waterloo. This claim has even been tacitly accepted by the Germans in what foreigners incorrectly tend to regard as their second national anthem, 'Die Wacht am Rhein' (The Watch on the Rhine). A silly British popular song of the early days of World War I involved the slogan: 'We shall wind up the watch on the

Der freie Rhein, songsheet, c. 1840. Poem by Niclas Becker (*left*).

9

Rhine.' This the British failed to do, just as in World War II they failed to 'hang up the washing on the Siegfried Line', though the West Wall was eventually smashed by the Americans in the final campaign of 1945.

As for Germany's eastern frontier, it has been fluid for centuries, an almost permanent confrontation, diplomatic and at times military, between German and Slav, with repeated partitions of Poland, with struggles between the Germany of Prussia and that of Austria for the formerly Turkish-dominated areas in what is now Czechoslovakia and further south. Today it is a matter of dispute whether or not the Oder–Neisse line is to be a future Germany's permanent eastern frontier.

So, not a geographical expression. The Nazis, of course, claimed that Germany was a racial entity. This is a quite indefensible simplification. The Prussians, whom Bismarck once described and accurately as 'the ballast in the ship of state', were very largely of Slav origin, as their names reveal, while East Prussia, now defunct, provided the hard core of German military leadership from 'a rooted garrison' of German conquerors and landowners who ruled over a peasantry of Slavs frequently not speaking German at all: in these respects they resembled the Ascendancy in eighteenth- and nineteenth-century Ireland. Hitler, one of history's 'terrible simplifiers', cut this Gordian knot by deciding that all who spoke German, provided they were neither gypsies nor Jews, were German. For military and economic reasons he did not make more than a covert claim for the German-speaking Swiss, but would probably have done so had his armies been victorious in World War II.

So, a linguistic concept? Again, this is too simple an answer, even if we leave out of account the Slav-speakers in the Third Reich's eastern territories, the French-speakers in Alsace-Lorraine and the polyglot elements to be found in Vienna. In Germany itself there are two languages and a multitude of dialects. The official language is High German, said to be best spoken in the Hanover area. But in north-western Germany the language of the people is Low German, or *Plattdeutsch*, which is closer to Dutch or even in some respects to English than it is to High German. (I heard, years ago, that in the Friesian Islands there is a saying, for the spelling of which I cannot vouch: 'Gud butter und gud tschiess ist gud englisch und gud friess.')

If the speakers of Low German were 'automatically' citizens of the Reich, then why not their close linguistic kinsmen in Holland? The answer is obvious, and political. When Hitler invaded their country it was not in order to incorporate it into his Germanic heartland: indeed at one time he considered transporting the entire population

Hitler Youth parade in the 1936 Olympic Stadium, Berlin.

of Holland to occupied Russia. Yet Dutch is merely the anglicization of *Deutsch*, and for many years the English referred to the inhabitants of 'the Germanies' collectively as 'Dutchmen'. There was an English lyric, again quoted from memory, that must have dated from two or three hundred years ago, in which there was a reference to 'the Potsdam Dutch and the Rotterdam Dutch and the Goddam Dutch. . . .'

If not linguistic, then certainly not religious. The Thirty Years War, that great traumatic horror in Germany's history only perhaps equalled by the traumata of Nazism and World War II, had resolved nothing, leaving Germany divided religiously between Protestants, mostly Lutherans and mainly in the north, and Catholics, mostly in the south and south-west. Hostility between the two faiths found political expression during the period of the Second Reich (1871–1918) and the Weimar Republic (1918–33) and has never entirely vanished.

So, is there a social homogeneity, comparable to that prevailing in Britain or in France? The answer would seem to be that this probably exists to some extent and has certainly been proved in the most testing furnace by German patriotism in both World War I and II. True enough, the clerks who work for a Hamburg merchant have little in

Watch on the Rhine. Painting by
Robert Geissmann.

common with, and may be even incomprehensible to, the labourers
on a Bavarian farm. But that is equally true of men from Devon or
Newcastle, from Lille or the Berri.

Even if definition is logically impossible, we all know, for better or
for worse, what Germans are, though foreigners' attitudes towards
them have passed through frequent, violent changes. The stereotype
150 years ago was the gnarled and aged peasant, 'and he before his
cottage door was sitting in the sun', fond of beer and music: or of the
philosopher-scholar poring through thick spectacles over his ancient
texts when not inventing archaeology or the modern sciences. We
have seen him, he has seen himself, as fantastically industrious and
obediently efficient. During and immediately after the two world wars
we have had another vision of 'the German' too well remembered to
need revival here. There is a considerable measure of truth in all these,
and indeed in other pictures of the inhabitants of a country which can
hardly be defined any better in historical than in geographical, linguistic, religious or social terms. Yet we all believe that we know what 'the
Germans' are. Our reactions to them may be based on ignorance,
prejudice and oversimplification. But we have none of us, including
this writer, any firmer basis from which to examine, even briefly as in
this book, their history.

Sunday Peace. Painting by H. Thoma, 1876.

Still from the film, *The Blue Angel*, 1930, with Emil Jannings.

Trip on the Elbe over to the Schreckenstein. Painting by L. Richter, 1837.

Landscape, near Ischl. Painting by F. Waldmüller, 1838.

CHAPTER TWO

The First 1500 Years AD

When precisely the proto-Germanic tribes emerged from Asia into Europe, pushing their Celtic predecessors before them and with the Slavs hot on their heels, is a matter for the speculation of scholars. Certainly it took a very long time, probably more than a millennium, but when Julius Caesar's Roman warriors had finally conquered Gaul, at about the time of the birth of Christ, they found the German tribes already installed in what is now Germany, a fierce, warlike and illiterate people, only beginning to progress from the semi-nomadic life of hunters and herdsmen in their vast, dark forests, to the practice of agriculture, still half Cain and half Abel.

The Romans tried, and failed, to conquer them. The defeat and destruction of three Roman legions in the year AD 9 under Quintilius Varus in the Teutoburger Wald, a range of mountains and forest roughly on the border of what was to become Prussia, was really the first major disaster to overwhelm Roman legionaries at the hands of foreigners since the Second Punic War, two centuries earlier. The enemy was principally the tribe whom the Romans called the Cheruschi, led by a warrior chieftain named Hermann (Latin: Arminius) who became, and has remained, a German folk hero. Though this humiliating Roman defeat by savages was avenged a few years later by Germanicus – significant name – who took his infant son, Caligula or 'Little boots', on his German campaigns, the Romans never again made a really sustained attempt to extend their empire eastwards into Germany. They contented themselves with colonizing the extreme western German territories, in particular those west of the Rhine. Garrisons of ex-legionaries were planted at Trier, Cologne and other strategic points where Roman towns were built. Roman methods of agriculture and viniculture (Rhenish and Mosel wines) were introduced, as was Roman law, and these pacified areas

Column of Marcus Aurelius. Detail showing Romans searching a village of the Marcomanni, A D 174.

Porta Nigra, Trier. Early fourth century A D.

Gallo-Roman funeral monument shaped like a Mosel wine boat.

have inherited certain qualities, certain modes of thought, which have distinguished them from the Germans further to the east, from that day to this. For the rest, the Romans, so long as they had an empire capable of self-defence, were prepared to leave the Germans alone in their forests (which in any case frightened and depressed the legionaries) while guarding the two main water barriers, the Rhine in the west and the Danube in the south. The Germans made occasional sallies, principally it is said in search of the wine they were themselves incapable of growing, and the Romans also accepted young German males as mercenary soldiers. In general there was, for some four centuries, little contact between the highly civilized and technologically expert citizens of the empire and the semi-barbarous Germanic tribes.

Thus, until the collapse of the western empire in the fifth century A D, the knowledge that most Germans had of Roman civilization was vague, very much second- or third-hand, and no doubt in a weird translation of language. (As for the eastern empire which lasted for a further thousand years, a solid and warlike salient of Slavs and Huns sealed this off from German intrusions, all the way from what is now Russia to what is now Yugoslavia.) Thus most of the Germans, contained behind Rhine and Danube, had only the haziest concepts of Roman law, of Roman or Greek methods of government, of Mediterranean culture, or, later, of Christianity. Worshipping, in it would seem a rather half-hearted way, a somewhat unattractive Valhalla of warrior-gods and their goddesses, they nurtured dreams of fantastically rich cities, built of marble, gold and ivory, flowing with wine and filled with beautiful white-skinned women. It was with such dreams that they poured across the Rhine and over the Alps once the buckler of the Roman legions had collapsed.

17

Mosaic in S. Apollinare, Ravenna,
depicting a palace of Theodoric,
c. 500–26.

Brooch with Latin inscription,
from tomb of Alamannic prince.
Seventh century.

Frankish stone cross from
Moselkern, Rhineland.
Seventh century (*far right*).

Barbarian horseman, relief on tombstone from Hornhausen, near Magdeburg, *c.* 700.

What happened to these people, who burst out of Germany, is not relevant to this text. Suffice it to say that like their descendants elsewhere, the conflict with a superior culture was, despite all the burning, looting and raping, a defeat for the initial conquerors. It took a few centuries, but in time the Franks from Germany became Frenchmen, the long-bearded Lombards Italians, the Visigoths Spaniards, and the Anglo-Saxons Englishmen. In due course, and in all these countries, they accepted in some measure Roman traditions, Roman law, the centralized state, and Christianity. Yet for several more centuries none of this penetrated the Germanic heartland, for those Germans who had gone seldom returned.

Charlemagne, who ordered the pope to crown him Holy Roman Emperor in the year 800, was the first conquering monarch to return to Germany, though not the first Frankish warrior to do so. There was already a Frankish royal castle at Aachen (Aix-la-Chapelle). However, these earlier incursions of the Franks, and especially those east of the Rhine, had been little more than raids with perhaps the principal intention being the neutralization of the heathen and perpetually aggressive Saxons. Whether this Frankish emperor was one of the new Frenchmen or an old Teuton it would be hard to say: probably both. Certainly his, and his predecessors', wars against the Muslim enemy in France and later in Spain had taught him, as a soldier, the extreme value of firm religious belief. This *revenant* led what would later be called a crusade, as brutal as usual, into the land of his ancestors, and forcibly compelled his now distant Saxon cousins to accept the Christian faith after the destruction of their horde and their chieftain, Widukind. Though an illiterate, reluctantly – for he tried to learn his letters in middle age, but was too old and no doubt too busy to succeed – he was very far from being uneducated by the standards of his day. Besides being a soldier of the very greatest brilliance, he was also an administrator of the highest ability, and a man with great respect for learning, which he strongly encouraged. From York he imported Alcuin to help him reform his court and clergy, and other experts were brought in or given rapid promotion. He encouraged the use of written records, in desuetude since Rome fell, and founded many schools and academies to produce the needed scribes and clerks, thus further strengthening the central government and creating respect for its laws. He spoke several languages, including very fluent Latin, and he took the Roman Empire as the model for his own. After centuries of chaotic invasion, petty warfare and

Decorative embroidered eagle from the 'mantle of Charlemagne', *c.* 1000.

Equestrian statuette of Charlemagne, *c*. 870.

brigandage, this promise of peaceful government was one of immediate appeal to most of his subjects.

It is doubtful if any but a handful of them understood the basis upon which Roman civilization had been based, and certainly less so in Germany than in France or Italy. His Germany, indeed his Europe, consisted of small, more or less isolated, rural communities, knowing little about one another and virtually nothing about the outside world, where the Byzantine Empire was the true heir to Rome and the concept of the *polis*, in fact as well as in name. Nevertheless the Carolingian Renaissance was very much a reality. (Is it pure coincidence that the Common Market of the Six roughly corresponds geographically with the empire of Charlemagne?)

However, his political ambitions in their widest sense scarcely survived his death, for administrative details were too complicated and the lines of communication too long in those days for the government of Germany to be viable from Paris or even from Aachen.

In 843 by the Treaty of Verdun the Franks seceded from the original empire, and the creation of what was to become a national French state, with a purely French king and a language based on Latin rather than German, slowly got under way. The Treaty of Verdun is an historical incident of the greatest possible significance. For over eleven hundred years Franco-German relations were to be, when happy, cultural with the French usually dominant, when unhappy, military. And the Germans were, in some measure and at some times, to be excluded from the mainstream of European development.

But only in some measure. From the very beginning the Carolingian Empire during its brief existence had left much behind it. The Germans had accepted and continued to accept Christianity, and this was constantly reinforced by the close relations that existed, through Austria, itself a German land partly Romanized, with Italy. An hostility towards the heathen, late Greek Orthodox Slav majority, to their east, led an increasingly civilized German people to become aware of their links with their neighbours to the west and south. However the still embryonic feudal concept, in its turn derived at least in part from the Roman concept of primogeniture, took root in Germany and, quite rapidly, a quantity of Christian dynasties replaced the pagan, tribal chieftains. This happened more in the southern territories, with their closer contacts with Italy, or in the west, bordering on France, than in the north-east, where Prussia and Saxony remained remote from all centres of civilization for many years to come.

The domestic history of Germany throughout the Middle Ages, though with certain idiosyncratic qualities of its own, was imprinted on the tribal past by the feudal present. German, as distinct from imitation Roman, French or Italian, towns and villages were built. For

Adalbert receiving bishop's staff from the Holy Roman Emperor Otto II (983). Detail from twelfth-century bronze door of cathedral at Gnesen (*right*).

example the Emperor Henry II founded the beautiful city of Bamberg in 1107, to be the seat of a prince-bishop. Indeed throughout the Middle Ages the rich prince-bishops, with an eye on what was happening in Italy, vied with one another in the glorification of God, and thus of their own priestly power, by the erection of splendid cities, magnificent cathedrals, and the decoration of these masterpieces by the greatest artists available to them. A specific and beautiful style of German Gothic sculpture and painting developed north of the Alps and east of the Rhine. The Carolingian Renaissance, and the skilled German craftsmen and artists whose ancestor it was, created a glorious and proud heritage for future German generations. Nuremberg was perhaps the most famous until largely destroyed by the bomber planes of World War II. Rothenburg ob der Tauber in south-eastern Germany is a fine extant example of the period. Some towns were walled, the gates closed at night against brigands and other potential enemies, and to this has been ascribed a tendency to provincial parochialism, which can produce on the one hand a form of xeno-phobia and on the other a sort of social claustrophobia – let me out of here! – which endured and perhaps still endures in the German unconscious.

Henry II holding a jewelled book of the Gospels. Eleventh-century miniature.

Speyer Cathedral, the east end,
eleventh–twelfth century (*far left*).

Nuremberg, detail from a
painting by E. Etzlaub, 1516 (*left*).

Rothenburg ob der Tauber (*below*).

Castle Eltz, founded 1157, in Rhineland/Pfalz, north of the Mosel River.

Cologne Cathedral, the nave. Founded thirteenth century (*right*).

As the Germans became more civilized, and more urban, they, like the Romans before them, came to regard their vast, dark forests as dangerous places, haunted in their folk-tales by witches and worse. From such emotions came much of the 'Romantic' *frisson* of the German eighteenth and nineteenth centuries which rapidly spread across Europe. The French, too, locked themselves up at night in walled cities, but there was a certain difference: the French were 'citizens', a concept inherited in transmuted form from Rome and, even more remotely, Greece: the medieval Germans had another heritage, and behind their locked gates and guarded walls were still in certain, subtle ways semi-urbanized tribes.

The picture of rural Germany, as the forests were felled and a more modern agronomy introduced, was again, superficially at least, not dissimilar to that of the rest of Europe. The feudal lords, descendants or successors of the tribal chieftains, built themselves castles, intended to be impregnable and frequently on mountain peaks. Here, surrounded by armed retainers, they could look down, in every sense, on the agricultural labourers below. One such laird, the owner of Babenswohl in what is now Austria, could say to these labourers, with impeccable logic: 'You will do as we say, *for we have the stocks and the gallows too.*' This form of forceful domination produced among those labourers a fearful respect for authority only occasionally broken by violent revolution against their masters. Feudalism in Germany was in general more ruthless, and more accepted by the underdogs, than in most of Europe. This, too, left its legacy, both of obedience and of revolution.

In the so-called Middle Ages, the Germans keenly embraced their comparatively new Christian faith. As towns became cities the great cathedrals were built, at Cologne, Munich and elsewhere, the greatest north of the Alps. The Germans took their religion extremely seriously – as indeed they have done all abstract, semi-abstract or at least non-practical ideas and ideologies – more seriously at that time than the inhabitants of France or of Britain, where religiosity seems on the evidence available to have declined in the centuries before the Reformation and its backlash the Counter-Reformation. In practical terms this meant that great political power passed to the prelates. A prince-bishop was precisely what his title implies, and though such potentates existed elsewhere in Europe, we associate the title more with the German than with any other religious hierarchy. This, too, endured, and at times most honourably. During World War II Count Galen, Bishop of Münster, could and did fulminate from the pulpit of his cathedral against the evils of Nazism, to the consternation of the Nazi leaders who dared not arrest him, while Cardinal Faulhaber in Munich was allowed to be almost equally if more tactfully

hostile to the all-powerful and allegedly omniscient semi-pagan totalitarian state.

During the feudal period there was a considerable spread of literacy, at least among the nobility and the still very small but growing mercantile and professional class within the towns. For this the Church was undoubtedly responsible, as it was for repeated outbursts of anti-semitism (again far from confined to Germany, but starting there violently with the massacre of 1096 and continuing as part of the 'Crusades' to come). After literacy comes literature. The Germans had, like most other peoples, their pagan bardic epics, of anonymous origin and passed down with mutations from generation to generation. Of these the *Nibelungenlied* or 'Song of the Nibelungs' is the best known, eventually to be glorified by the music of Richard Wagner. It was an epic of general Nordic origin, and it was in fact to the Scandinavian and not so much the German versions that Wagner rather curiously returned. Staunch German patriots have compared these rather confused legends of Odin and Thor, of Siegfried and Isolde

Row of prophets, *c.* 1225, from a relief in Bamberg Cathedral.

Crucifix known as a 'Plague Cross', fourteenth century.

and all the rest of the enormous cast, semi-divine and semi-mortal, with the cool, clear works of Homer and with that magnificent, also anonymous, early French epic, the *Chanson de Roland*. Medieval German literature was as provincial – in that it was written for and heard by a 'local' public – as was that of England, for apart from a certain French influence there were few cultural contacts at any but the highest literary level. Probably no more Germans read Chaucer or *Piers Plowman* than Englishmen read Eschenbach's *Parzival* or Strassburg's *Tristan*. But then art, whether literary or visual or musical, should never be regarded as some sort of competition, though comparisons between various cultures and periods can be enlightening. Yet since all such comparisons are highly suspect, this writer will merely remark that German literature in any modern sense began with the *Minnesinger* of the twelfth and thirteenth centuries.

These beautiful lyrical poems, of which the principal theme was courtly love, usually of the knight for his mistress but also embracing

Two miniatures from the fourteenth-century *Minnesinger* MS. *Left*, Wolfram von Eschenbach; *right*, Konrad von Altstetten.

the fields of religion and of politics, were directly inspired by the troubadours of Provence. However in some respects the *Minnesinger* were even finer, more sincere and more moving poets than their Provençal teachers. As lyric poets the Germans have, throughout the centuries and until this one, produced a large quantity of magnificent poetry, perhaps only and only perhaps, surpassed by their distant Anglo-Saxon cousins in England.

However, throughout the Middle Ages and indeed into quite modern times, they did not produce a writer of sustained literary genius and profound thought comparable to Chaucer or Dante, to Rabelais or Shakespeare, to Montaigne or Milton. It was not until the appearance of Johann Wolfgang von Goethe (1749–1832) that a German genius of their amazing calibre – and some might say the greatest of them all – came to enlighten, indeed to implant his very German views upon, the whole of European thought and culture.

It was much the same in the plastic arts, though here the development, if that be the correct word, was quicker. As in the rest of Europe, medieval art was almost entirely of religious inspiration

Madonna with two kneeling kings.
Painting by Stefan Lochner, 1440.

whether in painting, sculpture or architecture, when the last named was not a branch of military technology, as with the castles and walled towns. Charming and beautiful though many of their earliest paintings and carvings may be, they were not innovators and produced no contemporary comparable to Giotto or Nicola Pisano, though there were very fine schools of painting in Soest, Westphalia, and particularly in Cologne, in the late Middle Ages. Most of these painters are anonymous, being usually referred to as the Master of this or that locality, but Stefan Lochner (active 1442–51), whose paintings hung in Cologne Cathedral, is generally accepted as a forerunner of Albrecht Dürer. Only with the Renaissance, easier communications,

Albrecht Dürer, self-portrait, 1498.

and thus under the influence of Italy, and of a cross-fertilization with the artists of the Low Countries, did Germany have such glorious painters as Dürer and Holbein, transitional figures between the Gothic and the Renaissance such as Mathias Grünewald, Lucas Cranach and the sculptor Tilman Riemenschneider, to name but five men of genius, all of whom worked mainly in the early sixteenth century. They left few heirs, though this was in part due to the Thirty Years War, which will be discussed later in this book.

Throughout the Middle Ages external affairs, so far as Germany or the Germanies were concerned, were largely expansionist, southwards and eastwards, for a usually unified and powerful France prevented expansion to the west, Spain was too far away, while England had already been conquered by Germanic tribes and lay safe behind its protecting seas. Less forceful, less 'youthful' and perhaps less ruthless than the Normans, there were still enough younger sons of the German nobility to dream their ancestors' dreams of conquest and plunder and to look at a rich, disunited Italy and at the primitive peoples to their east, already spoliated by Tartars and Manchus. In the first case it was wealth and luxury that they wanted: in the second, land.

Centre-piece of the Heiligblut-altar, St Jakobskirche, depicting The Last Supper by Tilman Riemenschneider, 1518.

Holy Roman Emperor Louis IV (Wittelsbach) endowing the Grand Master of the Teutonic Order with Lithuanian lands. Fourteenth century MS.

Henry IV imploring Matilda of Tuscany and Abbot Hugh of Cluny to intercede for him with Pope Gregory. Detail from early twelfth-century MS.

Frederick Barbarossa with his sons, Henry VI and Frederick of Swabia. *Fulda* MS, *c.* 1180 (*right*).

There were times when Germans of various sorts controlled, or thought they controlled, most of Italy, the Guelphs among others in the north, the great Hohenstauffen dynasty (1138–1268) from southern Germany, establishing a kingdom as far south as Sicily, with a court of then almost unimaginable luxury and elegance and, if reports be true, of vice.

The names of Frederick Barbarossa (1152–90) and of another emperor, Frederick II (1212–50) known as *Stupor Mundi* or the 'Wonder of the World', became legendary, the former even mythical. 'He is not dead, he sleepeth', to awaken when his country needs him. And from their Sicilian base, with Italy and Germany behind them, these powerful, usually very competent and often highly cultured men were able to play a very prominent part in Christian Europe's crusades against the Muslim East. However, these German magnates came into direct confrontation with the papacy which, though weak militarily compared to the German invader, had other weapons at its disposal, both social and spiritual. The phrase 'going to Canossa' has passed into common usage everywhere. It was there, in 1077, that the German emperor, Henry IV, begged on his knees in the most humiliating terms for forgiveness after a political altercation concerning the investiture of clergy. Furthermore, and as is usual in history, the German invaders found themselves culturally incompetent to stand up against the Italians. Here once again, and not for the last time and not for the Germans alone, the conquerors were rapidly defeated and ingurgitated by the conquered. This, incidentally, is a lesson that the Russians of our own day appear to have learned: military power without cultural superiority is simply not enough, for armies melt away when rape softens into domesticity. As Bonaparte once remarked, you can do anything with bayonets except sit on them.

The Germans played a big part in the crusades, more prominent than that of the Spaniards, involved in their own internal crusade against the Moors, less so usually than that of the better organized and more centralized French, the German contribution to these ventures being comparable perhaps to the role played by the English. German knights joined the various quasi-religious knightly orders, Templars, Hospitallers and so on. They lent willing hands and strong sword-arms in the looting of the East, including Christian Byzantium in 1203–4, and in the forcible if transitory conversion of conquered Muslims. They too built castles, but unlike the French they did not attempt, successfully if only temporarily, to establish colonies *outre-mer*. In this endeavour the Spaniards, and later the English, were to copy the French in the so-called 'New World', in the Americas and along the fringes of Africa and Asia, and in this endeavour by Renaissance man, armed with superior military technology and spiritually equipped with the cross or crucifix, the Germans again took almost no part until as late as the second half of the nineteenth century. German colonialism beyond the seas was always a somewhat half-hearted affair, compared to that of France, Spain, England and even of their Dutch cousins. It may be because they had no heritage from Rome: it would seem more probable that geography, and the ill-defined and fluid eastern frontier of the Teutonic territories provided a greater incentive. Nevertheless the eastward thrust, that was later to be called the *Drang nach Osten*, which really began nearly a thousand years ago and which has only been halted in its periodicity by occasional victories of Slav over Teuton (the last being in 1945), has remained, as near as anything, a constant in Germany's history. It involved a basic, some would say an unnatural, reversion of the old German tribes' migratory tradition, westwards, with the West now blocked by their very remote and culturally very different cousins, the Franks and the Anglo-Saxons. It was, however, very directly an inheritance of the crusades, with their twin motives of compulsory conversion and territorial confiscation. And indeed its first, most dangerous and most traumatic practitioners were themselves directly derived from the Palestinian crusaders, a formidable body of men, half-priest and half-warrior, the armed might of the prince-bishop concept, the Order of the Teutonic Knights. They were only one of the knightly orders, some German, some foreign, some international, that were then springing up. Yet, so far as Germany's future history was to go, their highly spectacular career may be taken as symbolic, though it would be an error to regard them as representative of the German people as a whole either then or later.

Though probably in existence at an earlier date, the first firm record that we have of them dates from the Third Crusade, during the gore

Tannhäuser dressed as a Teutonic knight. *Minnesinger* MS, *c.* 1300 (*left*).

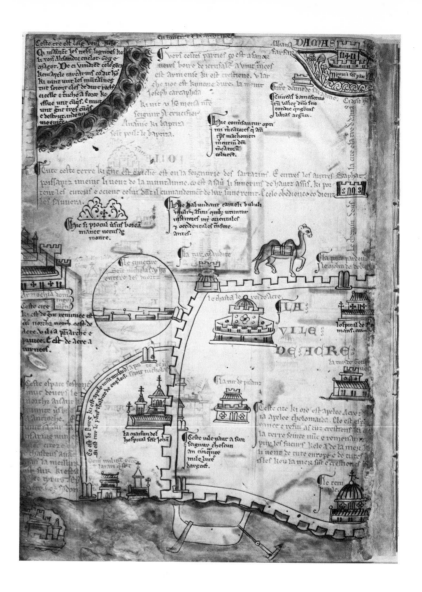

Map of Acre. MS from *Historia Anglorum*, before 1259.

and plague that made the Siege of Acre in 1189 one of the vilest incidents in that terrible series of campaigns. Taking over from the German Hospital of St Mary the Virgin in Jerusalem, and financed largely from the great towns of Bremen and Lübeck, the German Hospitallers were given their own knightly order in 1198. Dedicated to the relief of sickness and suffering, a role the Order never entirely abandoned, it soon became a sort of élite military club with a strong homosexual tinge and great temporal powers in the no-man's-land on the borders of Christendom.

After a century in the Near East, the Teutonic Order briefly moved its headquarters to Venice. In 1300 Venice was the commercial

Marienburg Castle, seat of the
Grand Master of the Teutonic Order
from 1309.

capital of the Mediterranean, indeed after the sacking of Byzantium
by the crusaders in the previous century, an operation for which Venice
had in part paid, perhaps of all Europe. The Teutonic Knights
learned much from the Venetian plutocrats and by the time they
moved their headquarters to Marienburg on the Vistula in 1309 with
mandates from various monarchs to Christianize (i.e. colonize) eastwards – they had already conquered Prussia – not only were they a
formidable military force but also an extremely rich and usually
highly efficient commercial and administrative enterprise. A century
later this military plutocracy was in decline, rift by schism and even
defeated by the Poles in 1410. Its power gradually passed into the

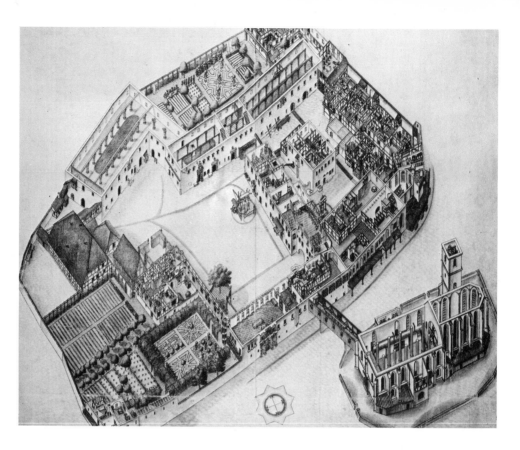

Diagrammatic plan of the living quarters of the Knights of the Teutonic Order, by Hans Bien, 1625.

hands of the Hohenzollern dynasty, who became margraves of Brandenburg, kings of Prussia, and finally emperors of Germany. Yet with its power the Hohenzollerns also inherited many of the Order's military-economic techniques, its expansionist policies eastwards, and even many of its militarist-plutocratic vices. These, indeed, outlived the Hohenzollerns themselves and bore what one hopes was their last, hideous fruit in Hitler's Germany. The formative importance of the Teutonic Knights, and of the other orders of chivalry in medieval Germany, particularly in the East, can scarcely be overemphasized, while the legacy they left behind them, though not altogether evil – loyalty, after all, is generally regarded as a virtue – was far from good.

The creation of modern Germany, that is to say the search by the Germans for a national identity, was to be in due course complemented on the one hand in the spiritual field, and on the other complicated in the socio-political, by the sermons and teachings of Martin Luther who, on 1 November 1517, nailed his ninety-five theses, most of them denouncing the Italian-dominated hierarchy, to the door of his church in Wittenberg.

CHAPTER THREE

Religious Conflict in the Sixteenth and Seventeenth Centuries

The Reformation in Germany and the Counter-Reformation were nasty, brutish and long. It was not until 1648 that the Treaty of West-phalia put an end to the killings, in the name of Christianity, that had culminated in the Thirty Years War, perhaps the most savage and protracted civil war that Europe has ever seen. There are no reliable statistics available, but historians generally agree that about one-third of the population of Germany was exterminated by other Germans and by the foreigners, such as the Swedes, who sought financial and territorial as well as 'spiritual' gain by sending armies into the ravished and chaotic land.

The allegedly religious, but in fact quasi-ideological, torments of a century and more ruined Germany temporarily, and produced certain social and psychological phenomena of apparently permanent effect upon the majority of the Germans. (Austria, being solidly Roman Catholic, was far less affected by the Reformation and its conse-quences: it developed into a different country, with different modes of thought and manners of behaviour from the rest of 'the Germanies': so too did the German Swiss, almost equally solidly Protestant. There-fore from the Reformation onwards these two groups of German-speakers will be tacitly omitted from what follows.) Two events, one at the very beginning and one at the very end of the long religious struggle in Germany, are both typical and of very great significance.

Martin Luther's thunderous oratory caused intense turmoil in Germany. Many of the priesthood followed him and some of the religious orders began to dissolve. The Holy Roman Emperor, Charles V, summoned the Diet of Worms (1521) at which he denounced the Reforms but at which Luther won a personal victory.

Wittenberg, the town church where Luther's 95 theses were nailed to the door in 1517. Woodcut by Lucas Cranach the Elder.

Paintings by Lucas Cranach the
Elder.
Left, Martin Luther, 1525.
Below, The three Saxon Electors,
Frederick the Wise, John the
Steadfast and John Frederick.

Emperor Charles V. Portrait by
Christoph Amberger (1500–61).

The majority of the Germans sided with him against the emperor and
the old hierarchy. Lines were hardening. Eight years later, at the Diet
of Speyer, the emperor ordered all the Reforms dismantled: this order
was almost everywhere ignored. The protestation of the evangelical
princes and fourteen cities of the empire gave Luther's followers the
name of Protestant, soon to be extended to all those new forms of the
Christian faith which, in greater or lesser measure (Luther in lesser),
rejected the doctrines and above all the authority of the Church of Rome.
Meanwhile, the great Peasants' Revolt had occurred.

The German peasantry in the later Middle Ages was not particularly
downtrodden by the standards of the age. Nevertheless their status as
villeins was very close to that of serfs and showed even less signs of
progress towards freedom than did that of their contemporaries in
England and France. Throughout the fifteenth century several
attempts at rebellion had been crushed. The Peasants' Revolt of 1525
was in part due to the illiterate peasantry's inability to understand the
ecclesiastical and doctrinal reforms desired and being achieved by the

43

On Aplas von Rom
kan man wol selig werden
durch anzaigung der götlichen
hailigen geschryfft.

Lutherans. Perhaps the most misunderstood statement was that of Martin Luther himself: 'A Christian is a free lord of all things, and subject to no man.' He was speaking in purely theological, not social or political, terms and, when the peasantry rose, he came down firmly and immediately against the rebellion, thus depriving them at once of the great moral support on which their leaders had doubtless been relying.

Those leaders – with the exception of the great Ulrich von Hutten, perhaps the finest German scholar and humanist of the age – were themselves a slightly suspect class, swordsmen and members of the petty nobility, who found themselves being squeezed out of their privileges by the growing power of the great territorial magnates on the one hand and by the rising influence of the burghers, the new middle class, in the cities on the other. Goethe, in his somewhat nihilistic youthful period, was to make a dramatic hero of Götz von Berlichingen, but characters such as Götz and Florian Geyer were

Ulrich von Hutten. Woodcut by Erhard Schoen, *c.* 1520.

already becoming anachronisms in the world of the Renaissance. Men of the sword, *condottiere*, were not always easy to distinguish from brigands when leading bands of armed peasants intent on plunder and loot in their search for a new and juster society. On the other hand Thomas Münzer, born in 1485 and executed in 1525, foreshadowed emotions and even events in the then far distant future. An Anabaptist, he was not only a religious but also a social revolutionary, an egalitarian, almost a proto-Communist, and a leader of men. It is not surprising that the Marxists have claimed him, even as they have claimed Spartacus and others, as a spiritual-political forebear, though these claims do not bear close examination. His followers under Johann Bockelsohn of Leyden seized and held Münster and the neighbouring lands from 1534 to 1535. Property was briefly redistributed and 'enemies of the people' done to death. This was the first real social revolution in German history, the rest of the Peasants' Revolt being in reality little more than a *jacquerie*.

The authorities, Catholic and Protestant alike, reacted as might be expected. Not only did they have the stocks and the gallows: they had armed men and the money with which to hire more. With great brutality the Peasants' Revolt was utterly crushed. Feudalism was clamped down, more firmly than ever, upon the necks of the peasantry. The peasants were taught to fear their rulers, the *Obrigkeit*, a fear which sometimes verged on veneration in the centuries to come. Only with the peasantry utterly cowed could their masters return to their own mutual quarrels about religion and land which reached a climax in the Thirty Years War.

The ending of that stalemate war, in 1648 after much horror, produced the second, significant hardening of a pattern that already existed. The Treaty of Westphalia had as one of its principal clauses the very important phrase, first devised during the negotiations for the Treaty of Augsburg (1555) but now extended and given a much greater significance, 'cujus regio, ejus religio', which in clumsy English might be translated as 'the regime's religion is that of the people'. This meant, in effect, that if the ruler were a Catholic so were the people over whom he ruled, and of course in the case of a Protestant ruler vice versa. It was quite an ingenious way to cut the Gordian knot of religious strife that had caused such misery for so long. It had one advantage: the individual was not usually victimized personally for his beliefs by his former enemies. On the other hand that individual, who, if he were a peasant had already been deprived of his aspirations to temporal freedom, was in large measure denied religious identity as well. The *Obrigkeit*, Protestant or Catholic, knew best. The prince-bishop concept, the claim of the many, petty (and the few not so petty) rulers to complete authority was thus institutionalized in the search for

'Beast of War'. Broadsheet depicting the horrors of the Thirty Years War.

Siege of Münster, 1534–35. Engraving by H. Sebald Beham.

Ratification of the Treaty of
Münster, 15 May 1648. Painting by
Gerard Ter Borch.

Battle of Blenheim, 1704.
Engraving by Jan van Huchtenberg,
1720 (*right*).

peace, and sealed in the blood of a long and awful war. The peace of
the grave descended upon Germany, and lasted for almost a century.
Exceptional men, of course, emerged, but on the whole there was little
art or science, and only a modicum of commerce took place. What was
for France the *grand siècle* was for most of Germany a period of
introspective stagnation.

Politically the 'cujus regio, ejus religio' formula, since it also
institutionalized on every level the fragmentation of the country, made
the Germans virtually impotent, and this at a time when Tudors and
Bourbons had already turned Britain and France into great, centralized
powers. There was no German power, outside perhaps that of Austria,
itself preoccupied with Turkish invaders, that could resist the aggressive military policies of Louis XIV. True, the Battle of Blenheim that
marked his final defeat was won on German soil, but it was won by a
British army, commanded by the Duke of Marlborough, in 1704.
Only with the rise of Prussia and of the House of Hohenzollern on
former Slav lands, was it possible for Germany to become a great
power. But with a most unhappy heritage, political, social and
psychological alike.

Germany during the early seventeenth century, showing borders of the Holy Roman Empire.

CHAPTER FOUR

The Rise of Prussia under the Hohenzollerns

Prussia, *Preussen*, is a word that has become part of the stock-in-trade of the political conjurer. The armed and armoured men of the Mark Brandenburg were frontiersmen and therefore, if they were to survive, soldiers. The real creator of the *Mark* as a state and a military power was Henry the Fowler (919–36). His successors were also usually strong and capable men. The swords and guns that they had, in the first instance, used to conquer and colonize a heathen Slav population, were soon enough directed against Germanic neighbours, Saxons and later Austrians, until in the fullness of time these weapons became not only military but also economic and were pointed westward and towards the north. The culmination of this long process was Bismarck's creation of the German Empire, at Versailles of all places, in 1871. Its end, however, was decided by other foreign conquerors in 1945, when the American, British, French and Russian authorities said that Prussia had ceased to exist. For them, and for very different reasons, the idea of Prussia had become a bogeyman, a capsule word for all that was worst and most terrifying in German militarism, in the ideology of the *Herrenvolk* or master-race, in brutal aggression. In this prejudice they, the Allies of World War II and the mutual enemies of the following years, were neither quite correctly informed nor utterly mistaken. The phenomenon of Prussia – the greatest German state to arise outside the Roman *limes* and far from the later *limes* of the Roman Catholic Church – was in historical terms short-lived, with a life-span of less than three centuries. But it was construed, by the older powers and the younger power of Russia, as a threat to peace, which it was. Its strength was also invoked, at times by East and West alike, to help against other enemies. Prussia, solid,

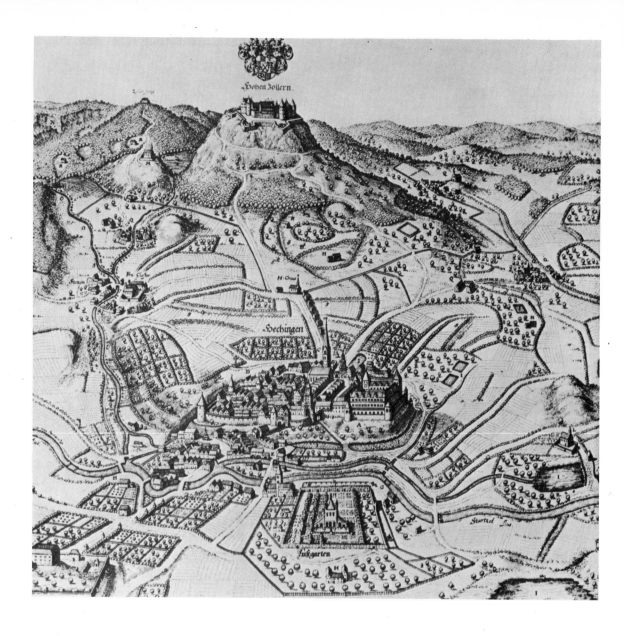

Hohenzollern Castle. From *Merian's Topography*, 1646–53

strong and unreliable, was to become in a way the sorcerer's apprentice in the shifting and dangerous alchemy of Europe's politics.

The word *Mark*, English 'march', implies a frontier territory, and this was certainly so of Brandenburg, an almost solidly Protestant district in the period that followed the Thirty Years War. The *Markgraf*, or margrave, who exercised total power in Brandenburg was a member of the Hohenzollern family.

The Hohenzollerns are not to be reckoned among the more attractive of the great European dynasties. From southern Germany

52

and claiming, as usual, an improbable Roman connection (in their case with the Colonna family which itself claimed descent from the Emperor Caracalla), its leaders served the Habsburgs well and were granted additional land, the Mark Brandenburg in 1415. This territory they proceeded to colonize, successfully, and became electors to the Holy Roman Empire. But it was not until the time of the Great Elector (Frederick-William, who took up the reins of power in 1640, that is to say shortly before the end of the Thirty Years War) that Brandenburg began to play an important role in German, and later European, affairs. He organized the territory's finances, played a clever political game, and created a powerful army, to be used as he saw fit. His principal territorial gains were to the east and north, into what was to be called East Prussia (thus outflanking the Kingdom of Poland) and to the Baltic coast. He also acquired territories in the jigsaw-puzzle of small west German states that were technically units of the Holy Roman Empire. However when he died in 1688 the basis of future Prussian power was firmly based on the Dukedom of Prussia, that is to say in East Prussia, a territory 'inherited' from the Teutonic Knights and never part of the Holy Roman Empire, as well as on Brandenburg, with its capital Berlin.

His son, a far less forceful ruler but a man of considerable culture, was elevated by the emperor to the status of king. The Kingdom of

Berlin, the royal palace.
Engraving by J. Rosenberg, 1781.

Coronation of Frederick I of
Prussia. Eighteenth-century
engraving.

Tabakscollegium of Frederick I of
Prussia in the Berlin royal palace.
Painting by P. C. Leygebe, 1710.

Prussia was established in 1701 and although in theory as Elector of Brandenburg and ruler of other imperial territories, King Frederick I of Prussia remained a vassal of the empire, in fact all Hohenzollern lands (which continued to expand) became integrated into the new kingdom. A major power was rapidly arising in Protestant, northern Germany. Vienna regarded this new, and therefore automatically *parvenu*, nation-state as unattractive and probably ephemeral. They were wrong, for they underestimated the Hohenzollerns.

The second Prussian king, Frederick-William I (1713–40), made a boorish impression. He was quite uneducated and totally uninterested in the graces of life, in the arts and sciences. His collection of enormous men, from all over Europe, to serve as his grenadiers, made him look ridiculous in the eyes of his highly civilized contemporaries and of history, and his brutal treatment of his son has become legendary. However he was not only a brilliant soldier, who defeated the Swedes and finally expelled them from German soil, thus further enlarging his kingdom, but also a skilled diplomat and great administrator. He made Prussia rich, and he used his country's wealth to create a superbly disciplined and well-trained army which was very far from being a mere spectacle of giant toy soldiers. This army, this wealthy and well-administered kingdom he passed on to the son he had despised and imprisoned, Frederick II (1741–86), who has gone down in history as Frederick the Great. Modern Europe, the Europe of the great states with their capitals from Moscow to Madrid, from London to Constantinople, was in existence. Of course there were to be many changes, but for two centuries the Great Powers, of which Prussia was now one, were to be engaged in power politics which may unfortunately not have ended even today. When Frederick the Great attacked and defeated Austria, he not only sounded the last post for the Holy Roman Empire (though it was Napoleon Bonaparte who gave it the *coup de grâce* a generation later) but also created a north German nation (though a further century was to pass before Bismarck could formally incorporate almost all the Germans into the new empire).

Frederick II (the Great) as a boy, dressed in grenadier's uniform.

Great individuals in positions of great power impose their characteristics, both those that they have inherited by birth or through society and those that are idiosyncratic, upon future generations. This is particularly so in the case of new, nascent societies. And no man had a greater influence on the German people's future history than the greatest of the Hohenzollerns.

His character was complex, in some ways perverted, and fascinating. He was extremely efficient, would never accept defeat, was dishonest as a diplomat, callous towards his own soldiers, ambitious in every way, politically, economically and culturally, vain and yet also

Sans-Souci Palace at Potsdam.

Frederick the Great visiting territories
at Rhinluch. Painting by
Frisch (1730–1815).

curiously timid. His taste was at times exquisite, at times atrocious. The two residences he built for himself at Potsdam would seem, architecturally, to exemplify this mild schizophrenia. Sans-Souci, his modest home, is among the most elegant European buildings of the Continent's most elegant century, while his palace there is heavy, vulgar and boring. He wrote what can only be described as fan-letters to Voltaire, persuaded Europe's greatest writer and wit to come to Sans-Souci, and then proceeded to insult him. 'I have sucked the fruit,' he is reported to have said, 'and shall now throw away the skin.' When Voltaire had a picture painted of a monkey throwing away a melon rind, Frederick ordered him out. Many years later, Alfred Adler, a Viennese Jew, originated the concept of the inferiority complex, an essential component to any understanding of the German character. Frederick the Great would seem to have suffered, and profited, from such a complex in a truly startling way. The Prussian state was to alternate between timidity and aggression, unsure of itself, of its legality, even of its methods though these were often highly successful. Prussia, and later the German Empire, were to bear the imprint of that great man who preferred the French language to that of his compatriots, even though Goethe and Schiller, Lessing and Winckelmann were publishing their plays and books while he sat on the throne of Prussia.

Frederick the Great visiting Voltaire. Engraving by Pierre-Charles Baquoy.

Frederick the Great returning from manœuvres. Painting by E. F. Cunningham.

Right, Johann Wolfgang von Goethe
(1749–1832).

Below left, Friedrich von Schiller
(1759–1805).

Below right, Gotthold Ephraim Lessing
(1729–81).

Left, Johann Gottfried Herder (1744–1803).

Below left, Gottfried Wilhelm Leibniz (1646–1716).

Below right, Immanuel Kant (1724–1804).

Students at Jena University, eighteenth-century watercolour.

It was not only in literature that the Germans achieved a sudden maturity during the second half of the eighteenth century, which was to be carried on by the truly beautiful 'Romantic' poets, of whom perhaps Hölderlin and Kleist were the greatest. In one branch of literature, philosophy, the Germans achieved a pre-eminence in Europe that was to be passed on for a century and more from the Prussian, Immanuel Kant (1724–1804) to Herder, Hegel, Fichte and Schelling, and thence to Karl Marx (1818–83). Perhaps no other country produced such a treasury of abstract thought as did the Germans of the eighteenth and nineteenth centuries, culminating maybe in Nietzsche, but spreading outwards to include the sciences: Einstein was a Jew, but the pernicious doctrines of Nazism must not let us forget that he was a *German* Jew. The German universities flourished, and indeed the whole standard of education was soon enough to be equal or even superior to that prevailing in the other great nations of Europe, with the consequent increment in wealth and power, which derive more often from skill and knowledge than from accident or conquest. Certainly there were many brilliant men in Austria and Bavaria, in Saxony and the Rhineland, where the Prussian ethos was not very popular. It is equally certain, though, that Prussia was the powerhouse, and not only in the political and military fields. This

60

University Library, Göttingen.
Engraving by G. P. Heumann.

'systematization' of German thought, admirably suited to scientific theory, also affected other fields of German thought and action, some-times most happily, sometimes less so. From the mid-eighteenth century, for example, a schematic approach to aesthetics from the time of the Enlightenment on gave German scholars a predominance in the history of painting and sculpture which they have never lost – or, if they have, then only recently to the Americans, who adopted many of the German thought-process methods, though melding these with their older, Anglo-Saxon traditions and French influences. Much the same can be said of archaeology, which the great German archaeo-logists such as Heinrich Schliemann (1822–90), the discoverer of Troy, transformed from a hobby into a science. War, too, the Germans tried to systematize through military theory, though in a far more subtle, flexible and far-reaching fashion than that of other military thinkers such as Krismánic or Bazaine. The great name here is Karl von Clausewitz (1780–1831). He had seen both defeat and victory in the French and Russian wars, and had meditated deeply on the reasons. He had also served as a very senior staff officer to Scharnhorst, Gneisenau and also to vom Stein, the real creators of both nineteenth-century Prussia and its steel backbone, the Prussian army, and thus indirectly of Imperial Germany itself. Most of his writing was published

Johann Sebastian Bach (1685–1750), aged thirty-five. Painting by Johann Kakob Ihle.

posthumously (1832–37 and later) and bears in English the title *On War*. These essays and studies of campaigns or battles were taken very seriously by the Prussian and then by the Great German General Staff, equally so in due course by foreign general staffs, less so, it would seem by the German generals actually in command of armies in the wars to come. In America particularly his analytical methods of discussing past strategy and tactics were applied with assiduity, while his much quoted apothegm that war is but the continuation of policy 'by other means' developed very sinister overtones. This great contemporary of Hegel managed to make a synthesis between the antitheses of war and peace with only three words: 'by other means'. Neither Napoleon nor Wellington in the past, neither Sherman nor Foch in the future, would have accepted such deliberate, clever rationalization. It was to have a powerful appeal, however, for certain elements within Germany.

In the most abstract of the arts, music, the Germans also achieved remarkable triumphs, from the time of Johann Sebastian Bach (1685–1750) until the present day. Here, however, the Prussian influence is less apparent, for neither Bach (a Saxon) nor Beethoven (a Rhinelander) nor Mozart (an Austrian) nor Wagner (a Bavarian) came from, or lived for any length of time in, that kingdom. Nevertheless, owing perhaps to the traditional encouragement of its superb orchestras and operatic companies of the highest quality, Berlin rapidly became a musical centre comparable to Vienna, Paris or Rome.

Only in the plastic arts, in painting and sculpture, did the Germans for a long time fail to recover from the ravages of the Thirty Years War. The centre of gravity in the Germanic, and indeed the whole Nordic, art world had at about the time of that war shifted westwards into the Netherlands, and there it was to stay so long as Holland remained a rich and powerful state. The great artists of the Dutch school were however much patronized by their German neighbours.

There were to be very good and very distinguished German practitioners of these arts, but nothing comparable to what had gone before or was to come in other European countries. There is no German Constable or Courbet, no Canova or Rodin, no Turner or Manet, and in modern times no Kandinsky or Picasso. The German Expressionists, interesting and often masterful, can hardly be fairly compared with the French Impressionists. It may be that the tendency of the Germans to concentrate on abstractions made them less susceptible to visual stimuli: a simpler explanation would be that the tradition of the great German Renaissance artists had not been allowed to take root.

In design, whether architecture, furniture, silver, even clothes, the Germans from the time of Frederick the Great were skilful, but with a

Pilgrimage church of Vierzehnheiligen, Main Valley, built by Johann Balthasar Neumann (1743–72) (*right*).

Porcelain group by Kändler
from the Meissen factory. Mid-
eighteenth century.

tendency to be imitative, in early years particularly of the French. In
the great porcelain factories, on the other hand, that sprang up in the
eighteenth century, usually under royal patronage such as at Meissen in
the Kingdom of Saxony or Nymphenburg in Bavaria, the Germans
had no need to seek models abroad, so great was their ability, elegance
and originality. In our ears the word 'shepherdess' is associated as
much with Dresden as with sheep. There were great architects, of
course, from Balthasar Neumann (1687–1753) to Walter Gropius
(1883–1971), and the Bauhaus group, who revolutionized twentieth-
century architecture, and not only in Germany. Yet before their time
it would be hard to define a specifically 'German' style of building,
though perhaps the elegant Berlin of Andreas Schlüter and Friedrich
Schinkel, built largely in the early nineteenth century, would be the
nearest. Alas, it has almost all gone!

On the mass of scholarship and scientific research that the Germans
produced between the time of Frederick the Great and that of Adolf
Hitler there is no need for further insistence. Nor did it cease with Hitler,
though under his brief rule the German educational system was badly
mauled, physically and ideologically, and in large measure 'research'
became racist and militaristic. However the period of Nazi misrule
and its aftermath lasted for less than twenty, not thirty years. There is
every evidence that the Germans in their laboratories and academies
rapidly recovered from this frightful experience, even as they did in
their factories, offices and shops. The artists, however, need deeper soil.

I fear that this long digression, into the arts and forwards in time,
too long and also too short, may have distracted the reader from the
history of late eighteenth-century Germany, as the growing power of
Prussia brought about an increasing polarization between Berlin and
Vienna. I shall return to a more chronological survey in the next
chapter. But it must be repeated that the Seven Years War, 1756–63,
which in this context was mainly between Protestant Prussia and
Roman Catholic Austria, sundered the Germanies irreparably until
the brief, Hitlerian hegemony of 1938–45. Two countries now existed,
for nearly two centuries, and it is principally with the northern part
that we are here concerned.

CHAPTER FIVE

Reconstruction and Development
in the Eighteenth Century

For Germany, as indeed for most of Europe, the eighteenth century was a period of reconstruction, or new construction, after the horrors of the religious wars brought about by the Reformation and the Counter-Reformation. In no great European community was there more to rebuild, nor a greater need for religious tolerance. The southern and south-western, and some of the western, kingdoms or principalities had rulers who had never receded from, or had returned to, the Roman faith. Most of the central, northern, and north-eastern ones remained Protestant. The split was, in large measure, fortuitous and to some degree irrational, but at least its tacit acceptance generally kept the peace.

Prussia had become the great Protestant power in northern Germany (for the Saxons had squandered their power in Poland and been spoliated by the Swedes), Bavaria the great Catholic power in the south with a love-hate relationship towards their fellow Catholics in Austria, while the Rhinelanders and their neighbours retained a fragmented independence from both these major German powers and tended to look to France.

Indeed the Germans of that century, those of the governing, intellectual or artistic professions that is, almost all looked to France for a model, for there was very little German patriotism and what they saw to the east of their lands they inclined, as they recovered and grew richer, to regard with a growing contempt. However the France that they admired and attempted to emulate was a country which was rapidly ceasing to exist, for it was the country of Louis XIV who had died in 1715 with his ambitions in ruins about him. Yet almost every German monarch attempted to build his own equivalent of Versailles,

Castle and garden of Pommersfelden.
Engraving by Salomon Kleiner
(1703–61).

Friedrich Hölderlin (1770–1843).
Pastel portrait by Hiemer.

some most beautifully, and to impose a rigid authoritarian administration on his subjects, often with more success, in the decades that
followed. The ideas that were coming into existence in France took
the Germans longer to digest. This is one of the inherent disadvan-
tages of copying foreigners' modes: the copyist is always out of date.

The great intellectual strength of the Germans had always been
manifested in the building of what might be described, rather rudely,
as imaginative cardhouses in which ideas are the cards. Nobody who
was not a German could have written *Faust*. Christopher Marlowe's
Doctor Faustus and the earlier German tale, in fact Goethe's own
youthful version, known as the *Urfaust*, quite lack the complexity of
his masterpiece and are, indeed, alien to *Faust*, Part Two. If he was,
as this writer believes, one of Europe's very greatest authors, comparable
to Dante and Shakespeare, he is also far more obscure in his mental
processes than his predecessors in greatness, and perhaps only to be
surpassed in the arcane by a later peer who came, significantly enough,
from the very outskirts of Europe, Fyodor Dostoievsky. What, to a
Western European, must appear to be a strange profundity or an, at
times, pointless obfuscation, was also manifest in Friedrich von Schiller
(who died too young to develop all the enormous talents evident in his
Wallenstein) or Hölderlin, one of Europe's very finest lyric poets, who
went mad too soon to develop his talent. The modern word 'neurotic'
is an oversimplification when applied to these great Germans of the
Classical-Baroque and even of the Romantic age. Yet, admire them

66

as this writer does, the appearance upon the German literary scene of Heinrich Heine, a moderately cosmopolitan Jew born in 1799 with a sense of wit and of proportion, comes as a relief. It is not unsurprising that the German literary gentlemen, the spiritual descendants of the eighteenth century, have regarded Heine with a strange mixture of distaste and gratitude. In that world, too, the gates of the fortress-city are locked at nightfall. But the artists were retreating to their dark forests. They have seldom ceased to do so, periodically.

The German retreat from the Latin world, into forests and later into abstractions, made their cleverest men quite inevitably attracted by the novelties of what is called 'science'. Nicholas Copernicus, the Polish-born canon of the cathedral of Frauenberg, decided as the result of mental deliberations that the ancient Greeks were right and that the world revolved around the sun rather than vice versa. Although his theory, published in 1543, aroused the hostility of the Protestant leaders (the Catholics waited till 1616 to condemn Copernicanism), he was nevertheless regarded as an intellectual hero and still is. Paracelsus, a German-Swiss (1493–1541), who had a heathen belief in magic, transformed alchemy into medicine. This was probably a good idea and it is said that many of those clean white hospitals should bear his name rather than the saints', though some might think otherwise.

Social changes in the Germanies were so varied from district to religious district, and so subject to the will or even whims of local potentates, that generalization is extremely parlous. The towns, as they became cities, Berlin, Leipzig, Cologne, Munich, Hamburg, Stuttgart and so many others, produced a middle class more jealous of its rights than their burgher ancestors, and therefore more inclined to favour proto-democratic than autocratic government. On the other hand because autocracy, on the French model, was the accepted form of government, though tempered by the plutocracy of the old Hanseatic centres, by the theocratic powers exercised in the Roman Catholic states, and by the power of the military in Prussia, Saxony and elsewhere, the desire of this new, essentially urban, middle class for status was channelled, after wealth, into the civil service. The result was the creation of a body of officials, the *Beamtentum*, usually highly efficient and often extremely arrogant, that became one of the wonders of the Western world, though not invariably a beloved wonder. The heirs to these conscientious, hard-working, often clever men, dutiful servants of the state's rulers whoever those rulers might be, degenerated into Hitler's cold-eyed murderers and, by imitation, into the *apparatchiks* of the Soviet Union's Communist Party. The *Beamtentum*, usually honest and almost always obedient, gave little to posterity. Yet they provided a strong element to the cement of German nationalism, for

NICOLAVS COPERNICVS
Mathematicus.

*Quid tum? si mihi terra mouetur, Solij, quiescit,
Ac cœlum; constat calculus inde meus.*

Nicholas Copernicus (1473–1543), after a woodcut by Tobias Stimmer, c. 1587.

Statue of Roland, erected in Bremen, 1404, as a symbol of liberty and self-government.

Feudal scene depicting a whipping.
Eighteenth-century engraving.

after the chaos of their pre-history and the self-inflicted wounds of their
religious wars had healed, the Germans – or most of them – could
announce: 'At least we know how to run our own affairs.' A simple
extrapolation followed: 'and therefore we know how to run other
peoples'.' The other people did not always agree.

Another element in the cement was the social position of the minor
nobility, the landlords. As a result of what had gone before, the
monarchs gave their men of rural property increased authority over
their tenants in exchange for the splendours of military power. Only
an aristocrat, or at least a man with landed aristocratic connection,
could be an officer. His loyalty to his monarch must of course be
absolute; no doubts, and above all no criticism, spoken or even thought.
While the private soldiers, the descendants of those peasants defeated in
the sixteenth century, decimated in the seventeenth, and reduced to a
servitude unknown for centuries in the eighteenth, were not supposed
to think at all. 'Thinking,' the German sergeant-majors are supposed
to have said later, 'is to be left for the horses.'

Some years ago this writer was allowed to read Stendhal's private
library, then as I hope now the personal property of Signor Gentile, in
Florence. The volumes, all annotated by perhaps the greatest of French
novelists, included a sycophantic life of the Empress Maria Theresa of
Austria. On the last page Stendhal had written, in a steady hand:
'Puis vint Bonaparte.'

The French Revolution began in 1789, and five years later Bonaparte
was in Italy. Not many more were to pass before his armies were to be
marching up and down Germany, too, blowing her ramshackle,
illogical and unjust society into matchsticks. The great German
philosophers and artists of the age, from Kant, Beethoven and Goethe
on down, surveyed this spectacle sardonically. Other Germans felt
otherwise.

CHAPTER SIX

The Napoleonic Wars

The first French Revolution aroused little enthusiasm in the Germanies. There were, of course, a handful of German Jacobins, but to the upper and middle classes, and to the clergy of both faiths, the Terror was very much a reality. The arrival from across the frontiers of large numbers of French refugees had much the same effect, at least so far as the *Obrigkeit* was concerned, as did the arrival of Russian refugees in Western Europe after 1919 and of German-Jewish refugees in France, Britain and America in the 1930s. Something disgusting and dangerous was happening in a great European state, which surely should be stopped, if necessary by force. Furthermore Jacobinism, like its remote descendant Bolshevism, was proclaimed by its leaders to be

Capture of Regensburg, 1809.
Painting by Charles Thevenin.

Princes of the Confederation of the Rhine acclaiming Napoleon as their protector, 1806. Contemporary lithograph.

Napoleon receiving the deputies of the Senate in the royal palace, Berlin, November 1806 (*below*).

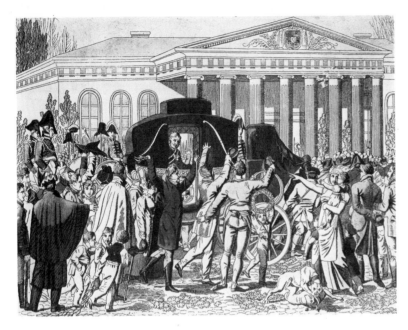

Return of the Elector of Hesse
from exile, November 1813.

an international ideology, marked clearly FOR EXPORT. Just as the
Western Allies attempted, and failed, to invade Russia in 1919, so
did the Germanies briefly unite with Austria to send an army into
France in 1792. It was not a very good army, and though it made some
progress within two months it was halted at Valmy (20 September)
and then rapidly thrown back by the forces of the French Republic,
created two days later. Until 1814 the armies of the French Republic
and later of the Empire did not have to fight on French soil. They cam-
paigned in Italy, Egypt, Spain, and finally Russia, but in the long
series of wars, only interrupted by periods of truce that could scarcely
be called peace, it was above all across Germany that they marched
and countermarched and it was against German and Austrian armies
that Napoleon Bonaparte won his greatest victories: Austerlitz (1805),
Jena (1806), Wagram (1809) to name but three of the more spectacular.

Socially the long series of wars seems to have had remarkably little
effect. There was no renewal of the Peasants' Revolt under Jacobin
leaders, though in the French-created and French-dominated Confederation of the Rhine the slogans about liberty, equality and fraternity
were repeated and the red, white and blue flag that symbolized
republicanism was saluted. In general, however, the German workers
and peasants obeyed and fought for their established rulers. Nor,
when the awful holocaust ended, did they show any marked reluctance
to a return to their previous condition, at least for a generation and
more, until industrialization began to produce a larger urban
proletariat.

Arrival of Napoleon and Marie Louise at the Tuileries after their wedding, 1810.

Politically, on the other hand, the tragic events of the long wars had had more immediate effects. The destruction of Prussia, at Jena, and the ultimate humiliation when the Austrian emperor was compelled to send his daughter Marie Louise into Napoleon's bed, produced reactions of expected violence but of a different nature. The Prussians, under the leadership of Count Gneisenau (1760–1831) set about the reorganization of their military forces and more important perhaps in the long run were the administrative reforms for which the major credit is given to Baron vom Stein (1757–1831) and to Prince Karl von Hardenberg (1750–1822). They had seen the Prussia of Frederick the Great so utterly humiliated by the French that German soldiers were compelled to fight, for the French enemy, against the Russians when Napoleon was running short of able-bodied Frenchmen. Though, with yet another change of allegiance, the Prussian generals and their troops deserted from the *Grande Armée* during its Russian catastrophe of 1812, and played a prominent part, culminating in the battles of Leipzig (1813) and of Waterloo (1815), in the campaigns that finally destroyed the First French Empire. Yet there was little national pride to be gleaned from the decades that had passed. Many administrators, and many philosophers such as Hegel, Fichte and Treitschke, were needed, in northern Germany, to re-create the steel spine of national pride, while Napoleonic humiliations led the Austrians to look the other way, into the Balkans and northern Italy.

72

The split between the German-speaking peoples of the north and south was thus accentuated, while Roman Catholic Bavarians, between those two great states, decided that they, too, must become a major German power. Napoleon had reinforced the lesson that Louis XIV had already and roughly delivered to the Germanies: power is what counts in politics. And the corollary to national power, indeed its prerequisite, is national unity. To such a unity there are three strands, the one internal and social, the other external, defensive or offensive as the problem of the day may decide, the third economic, which in the nineteenth century meant education and industrialization. After the defeat of Napoleon the Germans attempted, sometimes simultaneously, all three ways of achieving a national identity: at intervals they succeeded briefly. Perhaps at last they will happily succeed altogether. The history of this greatly talented, valiant and hard-working people does not however allow an outsider to foresee such a happy and desirable outcome within the near future.

Battle of the Nations at Leipzig, 1813. Contemporary engraving.

SWEDEN

DENMARK

Holstein

Hamburg

Mecklenburg

Danzig

RUSSIAN EMPIRE

Vistula

NETHERLANDS

Hanover

Berlin

Oder

Posen

POLAND

KINGDOM

Münster

Elbe

Cologne

Hesse

Saxony

Thuringian
States

RUSSIA

OF

PRUSSIA

Rhine Province

Luxemb.

Frankfurt a/M.

Palatinate

Bohemia

Nuremberg

Moravia

FRANCE

Baden

Wurtemberg

Bavaria

AUSTRIAN

Rhine

Weser

Munich

Danube

Vienna

EMPIRE

SWITZERLAND

Tyrol

Carinthia

Styria

HUNGARY

KINGDOM
OF
SARDINIA

Lombardy

Venetia

Carniola

250 miles

400 km

The German Confederation, 1815.

CHAPTER SEVEN

Expansion of Prussia in the Nineteenth Century

For the generation that lived between the final defeat of the French in 1815 and the second, major, French Revolution of 1848 it was in Germany, as in most of Europe, a period of retrenchment and indeed of reaction. It is artistically referred to as the Biedermeier period, distinctive for an elegantly genteel style of interior decoration for the homes of the growing middle class, with spindly tables at which they might sit on delicate and somewhat fussy chairs while they sipped their coffee or, less usually, their wine. Their other furnishings, their curtains, their pictures by Spitzweg and other late-Romantics, even

Family group. Coloured drawing by Friedrich Wilhelm Doppelmayr, 1831.

Karl Marx (1818–83), in mid-career.

Krupp Steel Works, Essen, 1819.
Contemporary engraving.

in some measure their way of life fitted into the same style. Respect-ability, combined with modest ostentation, was the aim of the German mercantile, professional and official middle class throughout the whole of the nineteenth century and into the twentieth. Perhaps the epitome of such sober modesty was the Prussian king who became the first Kaiser, Wilhelm I. It is said that even when Emperor of Germany he personally recorked unfinished bottles and snuffed out the candles before retiring to a solitary or conjugal bed.

Two vignettes might be said to mark the beginning and the end of the period between 1815 and 1848. The arrival of the Prussians under Field-Marshal Blücher on the field of Waterloo, in the nick of time, probably saved the Duke of Wellington's army from defeat. Later, when driving through London in some sort of victory parade, the Prussian is said to have remarked to the Irishman: 'What a city to plunder!' And in 1848 a German philosopher of the first magnitude, a competent historian, a skilled journalist, a most inept political prophet, and by all accounts a very disagreeable man, sat down to write *The Communist Manifesto*. Karl Marx's aphorism about 'the expropriation of the expropriators' had both the ponderous obscurity in its phrasing which Germans appreciate and the rather heavy social morality that they had come to relish in the nineteenth century. In a word, Marx made at least one aspect of plunder respectable.

Industrialization progressed rapidly in northern and western Germany. There was plenty of coal in the Ruhr area, and in Silesia

nach Aufhebung des Zollvereins.

Cartoon in *Kladderadatsch*, 1852, depicting Germany after an imaginary suspension of the Customs Union *(Zollverein)*.

there was iron, and, with an equally rapid growth in technical education, there were the technologists at all levels to exploit these natural resources. By the middle of the century Germany was producing the finest steel in Europe and the firm of Krupp, in Essen, was becoming a great concern. International commerce began to be very important, based mostly upon the northern ports. Internal commerce was even more so, and this was brought about by a series of very shrewd politico-economic decisions, beginning in Prussia in 1819, which extended the *Zollverein* or Customs Union steadily westwards, a sort of Common Market in miniature, which gradually unified all northern Germany into an economic unit. This was, politically, to incorporate southern Germany as well after 1871.

The westward shift of Prussian power, into the vacuum left by the defeat of France and the retreat of Austria, quite rapidly altered the nature of the Prussian state itself. Previously based in East Prussia and heir to the Teutonic Knights, it now became a west German power of great and growing strength. Into Prussian hands devolved the duty of the Watch on the Rhine. Prussian troops, and those of Prussia's allies, had to protect the Germanies from the scourge of French invasion, recurrent since the Thirty Years War. It must be stressed that at least until 1870 the confrontation between Franks and Teutons had been marked by French rather than by German aggression. And even when that war broke out many sensible, neutral observers in Britain and the United States saw it as yet another attack on Germany by France. By then, however, the new Prussia had completely changed the balance of power between the two nations. From that time France could not hope to defeat Germany without massive military assistance from allies, British, Italian, Russian and finally American.

While Prussia was steadily shifting its weight westwards, largely by economic developments and commercial agreements, in East Prussia little changed. The *Junkers* continued to cultivate their estates and to breed the great military families that dominated the Prussian and later the German armies, until at last the officer corps was in large measure destroyed by Adolf Hitler in 1944, and East Prussia itself was destroyed by the Russians in the following year. The names recurred among the generals and senior staff officers generation after generation, Schulen-burg, Arnim, Manteuffel, highly competent, brave soldiers, stiff-necked and usually of reactionary political views, not dissimilar to those Anglo-Irish military families, far away, across the whole breadth of Europe, which served the British Empire so loyally.

Events in northern and north-western Germany during the Bieder-meier period of industrialization and Prussian expansion were of only marginal importance to the Roman Catholic south and south-west. Wurtemberg slumbered on, and its governing class continued to speak French. In Bavaria the peasants continued to be peasants and to drink their excellent beer. Here, however, the ruling dynasty, which as usual in the Germany of the time set the style, was the House of Wittelsbach, and after the defeat of France the rulers of that kingdom tended, during the period in question, to look southwards, to their co-religionaries in Austria and, over the Austrian shoulders, to Italy itself.

The Bavarian royal family had profited vastly from the French Revolution and the Napoleonic Wars that followed. The seculariza-tion of Church property produced an immense increment to the State,

Watch on the Rhine.
German cartoon of *c.* 1840.

that is to say the royal, treasury. And largely with this money King Ludwig I of Bavaria was able to rebuild his capital city, Munich. He chose Renaissance Florence as his model for the architecture – and his architects did him good service – but the layout of Paris for his city planners: great avenues were created, with fine vistas between hand-some, pseudo-Italian buildings. The Munich that he created was a city very different from those springing up under the pressure of Prussian and Rhineland industrialization. It was to become, for a while at least, the 'artistic' capital of Germany. Elegant, spacious and quiet, its contrast to the new, noisy, garish cities of the north made it a most attractive home for German writers and painters in the later nineteenth century. A contented, or at least docile, peasantry ploughed the countryside: there were beauty spots, such as Dachau: mountains and lakes were within easy reach of the fine city, new and also medieval: what late Romantic could resist such a place? Who could have guessed that this would become the Nazi Party's own capital, *die Hauptstadt der Bewegung*, within a hundred years and then become the dreary, rebuilt provincial capital that it is today?

To go forwards for a moment, there was a strong strain of lunacy in the Wittelsbach dynasty, attractive to outsiders and to posterity, less so to their Catholic subjects. Ludwig I, he who built Munich, was a sort of satyromaniac. His infatuation, at a somewhat advanced age, with the Irish courtesan who called herself Lola Montez cost him his throne. Ludwig II, Wagner's patron and passionate admirer, was a homosexual who destroyed his nation's treasury by constructing flamboyant, neo-Romantic palaces, though he had inherited a perfectly good palace of his own at Nymphenburg. (Both these monarchs were perhaps the greatest patrons of the arts in an increasingly philistine country.) Ludwig III, the last king of Bavaria, was, quite simply, dotty. Had he had his wits about him, he would no doubt also have wished to encourage the artists. There were, of course, members of the family who were fully capable of carrying out their duties, and did so. But in a country such as nineteenth-century Germany was to become, the Wittelsbachs offered no competition to the Hohenzollerns, and the Bavarians continued, over their excellent beer, to grumble about the 'Prussian pigs'. This gave them, at least in England, a reputation for democratic respectability that they most certainly never deserved or earned, from the time of Ludwig I to that of Franz-Josef Strauss.

The steady and peaceful expansion of Prussia by commercial, industrial and economic means endured for half a century, from 1815 until the Danish war of 1864. The peaceful scene was only briefly interrupted by the unsuccessful revolution of 1848. Inspired as usual by events in France, or more specifically in Paris, in February of that

Hall of Fame, Munich, built by Leo von Klenze, 1843–50, with statue of 'Bavaria' in the foreground.

Design for Falkenstein Castle, 1883, by Christian Jank.

Tannhäuser on the Venusberg. Mural at Neuschwanstein by J. Aigner, 1881.

year, which led to the expulsion of the French king and a short-lived
Second Republic, the concept of democracy rapidly spread across all
Europe. The ideal that people should be allowed to 'govern themselves'
became automatically confused with nationalism in fragmented
lands such as Italy or Germany and among conquered or subservient
people such as the Poles, Irish or Hungarians. Although the urban
proletariat tended to support this essentially bourgeois revolution – at
least to begin with – Marx noted, with scorn, that it contained no real
economic content and therefore could not provide a new social
structure. In France the revolutionary *élan* quickly turned itself inside
out, nationalism predominated over liberalism, and in December 1851
Napoleon III proclaimed himself emperor, to the general approval of
most of his subjects.

Austria rapidly crushed the nationalist revolutionaries in its Czech,
Hungarian and Italian territories: the Danes crushed the German-
speaking population of Schleswig-Holstein, despite Prussian protest:
the Russians crushed their Poles, and the English their Irishmen. On
the Continent, at least, the concept of absolute government was if
anything reinforced, and in the view of the absolutists justified, by the
apparent total failure of the 1848 revolutions. However, the democrats had at least stated their case. On the one hand the most obnoxious
residues of feudalism, such as serfdom, were generally abolished: on
the other the possibility of a new form of government was implanted
in men's minds, and the autocrats knew henceforth that they needed
the approval of their subjects. For the next generation the principal
emotive issue of Europe's politicians was to be nationalism, but
democratic socialism was quietly strengthening its roots. Autocracy,
on the other hand, in a post-feudal society could rely on nationalist
populism and from that day to this has done so, usually with success,
in most European states: as indeed it is now doing in most of the
Arab states, Africa and elsewhere. Nationalism and populism were to
provide the real fertilizers for the soil that was to nourish Nazism,
Fascism, Stalinism, and the other forms of totalitarianism in the
twentieth century.

The 1848 Revolution in Germany had, as usual, its own idiosyncratic qualities. In the previous year Prussia's reactionary monarch,
Frederick-William IV, had summoned the Diet to obtain certain
agreements concerning commercial matters. The liberal members had
however insisted first on the voting of a constitution for the Prussian
king's realms. This demand was, of course, instantly refused, and
among the conservative deputies who defeated this liberal effort was a
thirty-two-year-old Prussian aristocrat named Otto von Bismarck
(1815–98). A somewhat older man who observed the developing
crisis was a serving officer in the Prussian army, Helmuth von Moltke

An Meine lieben Berliner

Frederick-William IV addressing his 'Dear Berliners'. Contemporary lithograph.

(1800–91), who was to become Germany's greatest general, a man of extreme personal and political modesty, certainly the most skilled European soldier since Napoleon and the star in the military drama to come.

When the revolutionary wind rose in France, the Prussian king, however, went into reverse. On 18 March 1848 he conceded freedom of the Press and gave his subjects a constitution. A vast crowd, mostly from the working class, assembled immediately outside the royal palace to thank their monarch. Troops were sent in to clear the square and, accidentally it would seem, two shots were fired into the crowd. The people turned on the soldiers, erected barricades, and there were two days of fighting with many casualties. Frederick-William, with a remarkable prudence that probably saved him his throne, then with-drew the troops from Berlin. He, too, 'went to Canossa', for on 21 March he let himself be seen by his 'dear Berliners' (as he addressed them) draped in the colours of the revolution, red, black and gold, and made an ambiguous, indeed unnecessary, statement to the effect that Prussia was 'merged into Germany'.

For at the same time a sort of parliament had assembled in Frank-furt's St Paulskirche. It was not an elected parliament, but represented the liberal bourgeoisie, in commerce and the professions, from most parts of Germany, with a heavy component of university professors. Its demands, apart from the usual clichés about human rights, were two-fold. On the one hand the demand for a constitution: on the other national unification. At first it proposed as monarch for this new state – the creation of which was certain to be resisted by many of the

The Frankfurt Assembly in the
St Paulskirche. From the
Leipziger Illustrierte, 1848.

German princes – a member of the Austrian imperial family, a certain Prince John who was believed to have liberal views. However Prince Schwarzenberg, who had succeeded the deposed Prince Metternich a few weeks before as the effective ruler of Austria, insisted that any Austrian accession to such an all-German Empire, a *Grossdeutschland*, must be as a unit, and inevitably the dominant one. The German liberal nationalists did not wish to be ruled by a power that was at that very moment suppressing by force of arms other liberal-nationalists in Bohemia, Poland, Italy, Hungary and Croatia; nor did they wish to see these foreigners incorporated into the ideological, linguistically defined, Germany of which they dreamed.

They therefore opted for a 'small German' solution, and turned to Prussia. However the Prussian king, despite his already quoted remark and his parade in revolutionary colours, had no intention of receiving an emperor's crown from what he regarded as revolutionary hands. Even had his ambitions, for himself and the House of Hohenzollern, been as overweening as those of Napoleon Bonaparte, he must have realized that were he at that moment of history to attempt the unifica, tion of all Germans, against the wishes of many of the other princes and potentates, including Austria, he would need to use force which could only be provided by a mass revolutionary movement such as he had just seen battling his own troops in Berlin. And he knew from recent French history that such a sorcerer's apprentice is likely to throttle the sorcerer once it has the strength to do so. It was therefore neither in his interest nor in that of his dynasty then to engage upon the adventure of empire.

He was shrewd, by the political standards of that or any other age only moderately dishonest, and he kept his throne. The revolution subsided, to be succeeded as usual by a period of reaction, and Prussia continued to expand in power. The crown and its apparatus of soldiers and civil servants, which now had to take a parliament into account, was greatly strengthened by the king's apparent acceptance of popular opinion and became, indeed, even more worshipped than before among the majority. Frederick-William IV was perhaps the most skilful practitioner of *Realpolitik* apart from Bismarck that Germany produced in the two centuries that separated Frederick II from Adolf Hitler. He was certainly of greater benefit to his country than those two. His people grew richer, and the young men were not killed in war.

Historians, particularly liberal historians, are inclined to regret the fact that the aspirations of those worthy men assembled in the Paulskirche came to little, that a unified, democratic Germany did not arise at that time. This regret is quite comprehensible, but its corollary – that later German history would have been changed for the better – does not stand up to analysis. The immediate result would almost certainly have been revolution, an all-German civil war, vast loss of life and treasure, and some form of reinforced autocracy in an exhausted and impoverished country. All this, by devious means, King Frederick-William IV postponed for two or three generations.

It is said that the Prussian chief of staff of the period, General Otto von Manteuffel, was asked after his retirement whether he regretted never having commanded the Prussian army in a military campaign. His reply was that his only regret as a soldier was that he had not been allowed to conquer Berlin in 1848. This remark, too, is in retrospect an omen of things to come.

Germany 1871–1914.

CHAPTER EIGHT

Bismarck and the Unification of Germany

Bismarck, a name that sounded and sounds harsh in foreign ears, the man who once advocated 'blood and iron' as the solution to Germany's problems, who presided over the defeats of Denmark, Austria and France, the real creator of the German Empire, this Prussian aristocrat who cast a shadow across Europe of almost Napoleonic depth and significance, became one of history's bogeymen. This was a role to which he certainly never aspired and which he, with almost equal certainty, never deserved.

Born in 1815, some two months before the final overthrow of Napoleon I, he was as a young man a radical liberal. He became a civil servant in 1837, but that profession displeased him and he retired to administer his own estates in the following year, which he ran with extreme efficiency. This experience changed his political views and he was later to say that a country run by the working class was the equivalent of a household run by the nursery. He became a very clever conservative, determined that the methods he had used in his own affairs should also benefit his country and his class. He was elected to the Prussian Diet in 1847 and was one of the strongest opponents of the revolutionary ideals that exploded a year later.

Having made up his mind about the basic internal problems, economic and social, of the North German Federation which had resulted from the Customs Union (*Zollverein*), Bismarck turned his attention to two great matters: the unification of Germany and the new state's relationship with its neighbours, Russia, Austria and France. After serving as Prussian ambassador in St Petersburg and, briefly, in 1862 in Paris, he was in that same year appointed prime minister of Prussia by King William, who had recently succeeded

Prince Clemens von Metternich, the Austrian Chancellor. Painting by Thomas Lawrence, 1819.

his brother Frederick-William IV. For the next twenty-eight years, until his dismissal by the last Kaiser, grandson of the first, he was the undisputed master of the Germany he had done so much to create and which he transformed into the most powerful state in Europe.

Bismarck is frequently described as a reactionary imperialist. This is far from the truth. That he was, after the fiasco of 1848, an anti-revolutionary is certainly true, and he took as model Prince Metternich, who had ruled Austria so long and so successfully that he preserved the Austrian Empire from dissolution and maintained the Habsburg dynasty far beyond what would seem in retrospect to have been its natural span of life. But Bismarck was not a man to hanker after 'the good old days'. The reader who has got so far in this brief survey of Germany's history will have realized that there were no 'good old days'. The true reactionaries of his time in Germany were most of the princes and many of the aristocrats, both in Prussia and elsewhere. The new and ever-growing middle class yearned for a unified Germany, not merely for economic and even sentimental reasons, but also pre-cisely to curb these petty potentates and destroy their powers. It was on

Otto von Bismarck-Schönhausen,
deputy to the Landtag, 1847.
Engraving from a family portrait.

them, as represented by the National Liberals, that Bismarck in the
first instance relied.

In 1867, to win the support of the moderates, he drafted a new constitution, intended as a synthesis between democracy and authoritarian
rule. Henceforth the delegates to the *Reichstag* of the North German
Federation, and after 1871 of the Empire, were elected by direct,
secret and universal franchise. On the other hand the position of
chancellor remained a royal, later imperial, appointment. Thus the
Reichstag could and did criticize, and up to a point obstruct, legislation.
Unlike the members of the British Parliament the passing of an adverse
vote even on a major issue by the delegates did not entail the resigna-
tion of the chancellor and his government. Only the king/emperor
could order this. Needless to say the first chancellor was Otto von
Bismarck and though he was dismissed in 1890 the constitution
remained basically unchanged until the revolution of 1918.

To add further stability to the new German state which he was
creating, Bismarck on the one hand allowed the principal satellites
of Prussia to retain a sort of theoretical sovereignty and their princes or

Children's nursery attached to a factory in the 1880s. From the *Leipziger Illustrierte*.

Illustration describing the progress of German Social Insurance, introduced by Bismarck in 1885.

Die deutsche Sozialversicherung
steht in der ganzen Welt vorbildlich und unerreicht da.

Die Krankenversicherung

Altersversicherung

Jnvaliden-Fürsorge

Hinterbliebenen-Fürsorg

11 Milliarden Mark wurden in der deutschen Arbeiterversicherung-Sozial-fürsorge- in der Zeit von 1885 bis 1913 aufgewendet.

Krankenversicherung 1912 in	Deutschland	England	Frankreich
Beiträge in Millionen Mark	464	besitzt ähnliche	41
Leistungen " " "	426	Einrichtungen	24
Verhältnis von Leistung zu Beitrag	92%	erst seit Mitte	59%
Leistung pro Fall in Mark	65	1912	40

kings the trappings of power. But, more important, he quite deliberately wooed the working class. It was he, long before the French or British, who introduced the concept of 'welfare' into his legislation, with sickness benefits, unemployment pay, old age pensions and so on. This long series of legislation undercut most neatly the revolutionary opponents of the monarchical, quasi-democratic constitution until the disasters of the lost war of 1914–18 gave many of the German people a real grievance against the system: even then, they were in the minority and their revolutionary triumphs were both incomplete, localized and of very brief duration.

The army was something else which he, ably assisted by Albrecht von Roon, largely reorganized. To please the aristocrats, the officer corps of the regular army remained almost entirely the perquisite of their class and indeed this arrangement was reinforced. On the other hand a large reserve army was created, and in this the officers came usually from the middle class. Since there was great popular demand for a powerful German army – past invasions had not been forgotten – this was politically, both for internal and external purposes, a very

Krupp's Great Cannon, at the Paris International Exhibition, 1867. From the *Leipziger Illustrierte*.

shrewd move indeed. And when he had trouble with the Reichstag over money for this new, enlarged army in 1862, Bismarck passed a bill by which the authorization of payments was for a period of seven years, not once a year as in Britain. In those days this gave the staff officers ample time to plan, and to train the troops, against all foreseeable contingencies, in full knowledge of the manpower and equipment that would be available. And the Great German General Staff became the finest group of military experts that the world has ever seen.

In foreign policy Bismarck was a believer in *Realpolitik*, the politics of the possible. At first pro-Austrian, he was disillusioned by Austria's defeat by France in the Italian War of 1859, and was well aware that the Austro-Russian alliance had cooled almost to zero as a result both of Austrian neutrality in the Crimean War of 1854–56 and of the growth of Pan-Slavism both in Russia and in some of Austria's Balkan territories. Austria was, in fact, not a good horse to back, nor did Austria's historic claim to pre-eminence in the Germanic lands appeal to the Prussian.

Nevertheless in 1864, when there was a dispute with Denmark about the largely German-speaking territories of Schleswig-Holstein, Bismarck made a short-lived alliance with Austria, and troops both Prussian and Austrian defeated the army of little Denmark. A sort of condominium was set up in the territories. This was a totally illogical compromise and soon enough Prussia and Austria were at loggerheads. In June of 1866 Prussia, taking advantage of Austria's continued involvement in her war with Italy, seized the whole of Schleswig-Holstein and, a week later, Prussian troops also more or less peacefully occupied Saxony, Hanover and Hesse, though the Hanoverians later fought and lost a small battle. By then Prussia, or rather the North German Federation, was at war with Austria. On 3 July the Prussian army utterly defeated the Austrians at Königgrätz (also called Sadowa) and the war was over, with Prussia the master of all northern, eastern and almost all western Germany, and by means of secret agreements in close alliance with the states of southern Germany, too. Those latter, mostly Roman Catholic states, were very close to the Protestant tiger, which had now shown its teeth. A non-Austrian Germany could not be long delayed, except by defeat in war. Bismarck had also strengthened his country's position by close co-ordination with the Russians. His eastern front, he had reason to believe, was safe.

Bismarck was well aware that his western front was not, and the French did not appreciate this new and powerful federation that was straddling the Rhine. He therefore imposed a gentle peace treaty on Austria, intended to cause minimal harm to Austrian national pride – though territory was ceded – and set about the consolidation of the

Council of War, 1870. Painting by
Anton von Werner. *Standing, left
foreground*, Crown Prince Frederick.
Seated, Kaiser Wilhelm I, Von
Moltke and Bismarck, with Roon
standing behind him.

Prussian domains. (He did not send Prussian troops into Vienna,
any more than he had sent them into Copenhagen or was to have a
victory parade through Paris. He knew enough history to remember
the ultimate folly of such Napoleonic histrionics and display. Like
the king/emperor he served, and like the German General Staff he,
Roon and Moltke created, he was aware of the maxim: be more than
you appear!) He also attempted to encircle France by an alliance with
Britain, but here he met with a rebuff: the eighteenth century was long
past, and the British, safe behind their two-fleet navy (a concept
meaning a fleet capable of neutralizing or destroying the two combined
fleets of any combination of foreign powers), had no wish to be
involved in continental wars. Bismarck, like most of the politicians
of his age, believed in the dangers of encirclement and therefore in the
value of isolating potential enemies. With Germany now safe to the
north, east and south, Spain alone offered a possible, isolating ally
against France, and when a Hohenzollern prince was offered the
Spanish throne he was in favour of acceptance. The Emperor

Ho ch ·Hurrah· ·Preussen·

Deutschland!

Siege of Paris, 1870–71, Fort de Montrouge.

Napoleon III reacted violently and after an exchange of insulting messages, made more so by Bismarck's editing of the text, declared war. The south German states, but not Austria, immediately sided with Prussia and the Franco-Prussian War began on 19 July 1870.

The French army fought with great gallantry, but was hopelessly outgunned and outwitted by the Germans. With great speed and at comparatively small cost Moltke destroyed the main French army in eastern France and took many prisoners, including the emperor himself. He then proceeded to besiege Paris and occupy almost all the rest of France. Even before the armistice was signed with the provisional French government – in such humiliating circumstances Napoleon III had had no choice but to abdicate – William, King of Prussia, was declared Emperor of Germany at Versailles on 18 January 1871. Ten days later came armistice. Even while Bismarck was negotiating a peace treaty with the provisional government, headed by Louis Thiers, elements of the working class rose in Paris and declared the Commune. The Germans who ringed the city watched grimly while Frenchmen shot Frenchmen until at last Thiers had destroyed the Commune with much brutality on both sides. It must have seemed to the Germans that by Napoleon's declaration of war, his defeat, and now civil war in Paris, France had destroyed itself as a great power.

Heading from a war newspaper distributed at the front in the Franco-Prussian War (*left above*).

Wilhelm I visiting the battlefield at Sedan, 2 September 1870. After a drawing by Wilhelm Camphausen (*left below*).

Wilhelm I proclaimed Emperor of Germany at Versailles, 1871. In the foreground, Bismarck and Von Moltke. Painting by Anton von Werner.

Nor were they entirely wrong in their judgment. The only powers Imperial Germany had to fear, the one in the economic and naval field, the other in the military, were Britain and Russia.

Bismarck decided to further weaken France by a vast financial levy: until it was paid, nine French provinces were to remain occupied. In the circumstances this would appear a not unreasonable form, in modern terms, of the spoils of war. However he made one grievous error, which seems curiously out of character, in the annexation of Alsace-Lorraine, to which Prussia or indeed Imperial Germany had no claim save that part of the population spoke a form of German. The French paid off their indemnity with remarkable speed, far more quickly than the Germans had expected, for a major 'economic miracle' had followed the lost war and the failed revolution. Alsace-Lorraine was another matter altogether.

It was annexed for purely military reasons. Strassburg and Metz in French hands constituted a potential threat to all of southern Germany. For three years it was treated as a colony, and when it was truly incorporated into the Reich its delegates solidly and steadily voted against their status as a province of the Reich. The attempts at linguistic and historical justification for this seizure of French territory were dismissed, by Bismarck himself, as 'a professor's brain-child'. In France, however, such witticisms were hardly appreciated.

In Paris the Place de la Concorde is ringed by heroic statues in honour of the great French provincial cities. 'Strasbourg' was draped in black crêpe, and remained so until 1918, a symbol of the French desire for 'revenge' which embittered Franco-German relations for such a very long time.

Bismarck at Versailles, 1871, with Favre and Thiers. Painting by Carl Wagner.

Payment of the French War
indemnity. Arrival of a wagon-load
of coin at the Banque de France,
Strasbourg, 10 May 1871.

In external affairs, during the years between 1871 and his fall in
1890, Bismarck's major preoccupation was still encirclement. Germany was an extremely strong military power indeed, but the night-
mare of a war on two or more fronts haunted him, and rightly so, for
that was the virtual cause of Germany's defeat in both world wars of the
twentieth century. With France rapidly recovered, and clearly intent
on *revanche*, it was essential that he prevent a Franco-Russian alliance,
and he therefore established most friendly relationships with St
Petersburg. He avoided a quarrel with Austria, too, even though he
was simultaneously flirting with the Italians. It is said that geography
makes history. In the case of Imperial, and even of Nazi, Germany,
this means, in effect, only one enemy at a time. When this precept is
ignored, as it was by Kaiser Wilhelm II and by Adolf Hitler, that can
only in the long run mean defeat. Bismarck performed a diplomatic
juggling act of immense skill, and for a long time, while his country
remained at peace and became much stronger industrially, and the
German people were ever more integrated politically and socially into
the new empire.

If he made one grave error in internal affairs it was probably his attempt to weaken the powers, educational and ultimately political, of the Roman Catholic Church, the so-called *Kulturkampf*. As a Prussian Protestant bent on German unification, he saw no reason why the German Catholics should be, in any way, a state within the state. However, he was here venturing into a field where *Realpolitik* can seldom operate successfully. The result was the hostility not merely of the hierarchy but of a large proportion of the Roman Catholic laymen, particularly in western and southern Germany, and the formation of a Catholic political party, called the Centre Party, which grew rapidly and at times formed an alliance with the Social Democrats, who were also increasing in strength and who sat to the left of the Centre delegates in the Reichstag. Bismarck also quarrelled with the National Liberals. He had never been popular with the aristocracy, and by the time Kaiser Wilhelm I died in 1888, Bismarck's government was remarkably isolated from the elected delegates of the people. Despite this, however, during his long period in office he had supervised the creation of a very strong national state, the citizens of which were united in patriotism.

After a very brief reign of one hundred days by Kaiser Wilhelm I's dying son, Wilhelm II came to the throne. Almost immediately he

Cartoons from *Kladderadatsch*. *Left below*, The Triple Alliance (1883). *Right below*, Bismarck and the Pope discussing the end of the *Kulturkampf* (1878).

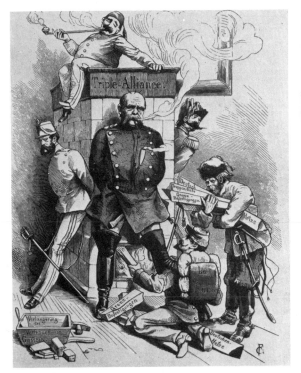

The repeal of anti-Socialist legislation in October 1890.

quarrelled with Bismarck, who openly despised him. The quarrel was dual. In domestic affairs the new Kaiser wished to extend Bismarck's social legislation in order once again to undercut the growing appeal of the Social Democrat Party to the now huge and powerful industrialized working class. On the other hand, since Russia and Austria were becoming increasingly hostile over Balkan matters, Wilhelm II decided to strengthen his Austrian alliance by a refusal to renew the so-called 'Reinsurance Pact' with Russia. Bismarck dismissed the first as 'sentimental clap-trap', and as for the second it meant consigning his life's work to the scrapheap, for that skilled diplomat foresaw, quite correctly, that the outcome could only be an eventual Franco-Russian alliance and thus the encirclement of Germany which he had fought, so long and so hard, to avoid.

DROPPING THE PILOT.

Cartoon from *Punch*,
29 March 1890.

Bismarck retired, embittered, to his estates, where he died in 1898. On his tombstone, at his own request, is the inscription: 'A Loyal German Servant of Kaiser Wilhelm I'.

One of the most famous of *Punch* cartoons, published at the time of his departure from office, was entitled 'Dropping the Pilot'. It was to prove more apt than the cartoonist could then have guessed. In the next fifty years the German ship of state was to veer in the strangest directions, and more than once on to the very reefs that Bismarck had known so well and had circumnavigated with a sure hand and a skill that has seldom been surpassed by any public man anywhere. The age of caution, modesty and consolidation was nearly over, to be replaced by an age of deliberate risk, flamboyance and adventurous activity.

Ballsouper. Painting by A. von Menzel, 1878.

CHAPTER NINE

The Wilhelmine Period and World War I

The Wilhelmine Period, that is to say the period dominated by the personality and policies of Kaiser Wilhelm II, lasted for close on a quarter of a century, from the fall of Bismarck to the failure of the younger Moltke to emulate his greater namesake as chief of staff by winning a rapid and total victory in 1914: but it may well be that the diplomatic ineptitudes and strategic misapprehensions of Germany's leaders throughout most of the preceding twenty-four years had put such a triumph just, but only just, out of reach.

Although the ever-growing might of Imperial Germany caused a certain apprehension all over Europe, which was to increase, the country that Bismarck had run had had no real potential enemies, save France, of any great strength. Even the creation of a small German colonial empire, in which the most important element was German South-West Africa (Bismarck accepted German imperial suzerainty in that territory from its 'owner', a Bremen merchant named Lüderitz) did not cause many flutters in the chancelleries of Europe. Even less so, in London at least, did the acquisition of the Cameroons and other Pacific islands and German East Africa. This was the great age of colonization and, since they scarcely possessed a navy, the German colonists appeared little more of a threat to the British Raj than did Belgium. If there were a threat, it came from the Russians poised on India's north-west frontier and steadily maintaining their eastwards pressure, which might be redirected southwards, from the French in Africa, and to a much lesser degree, from the United States, in the Caribbean, the Pacific and above all economically in South America, most of which continent, until early in this century, was virtually owned or at least economically controlled by the City of London.

Cartoon from *Jugend*, Munich, 1896, depicting German efficiency in Africa.

When Bismarck retired to Friedrichsruhe in 1890 Britain therefore had little reason to fear Germany while the Germans, or at least the German upper class, were attempting to still their complexes of inferiority by an emulation of the 'English gentleman', much as their grandfathers had tried to copy the French nobility. Was not the new Kaiser himself a grandson of Queen Victoria, a nephew of the next English monarch, Edward VII, of whom it is said that he preferred to speak German in moments of intimate privacy? Could not the two great Germanic powers, one naval, one military, both industrial, control the world between them? This was a German idea, which lingered on at least until 1940 and perhaps still lingers. It is one that appealed to only a negligible handful of Englishmen, for centuries of 'wooden walls' had brought about a contempt for almost all foreigners in the mass of the people. An inferiority complex can work in both directions. English gentlemen did not appreciate being told tactlessly that they resembled their German imitators: they were quite sure that they did not. Americans have, I think, inherited this particular and rather peculiar form of pride.

Royalty at Windsor Castle, 1907. *Seated*, Edward VII, behind him Wilhelm II, next to the future Queen Mary and George V.

Politically post-Bismarckian Germany alienated the British in many ways and by many acts or incidents, not all of which can be blamed upon the Germans. The rapid growth of German power before, during and after the Franco-Prussian War, and the alliances of the German Empire with Austria and Italy (the Triple Alliance of 1882) had fundamentally altered the balance of power in Europe, and it was on this balance that British isolationism from European affairs had long been based. As Germany grew stronger and stronger (to give but two examples, the production of coal multiplied almost ninefold between 1870 and 1913, while that of pig-iron increased from less than 1·5 million metric tons to close on 17 million in the same period) 'splendid isolation' became a memory, for without the prospect of active British intervention the balance of power had ceased to exist.

Furthermore two events, the one of ephemeral political importance, the other of the greatest strategic significance, had done much to alienate British sympathy, even affection, for the new, efficient, technologically admirable Germany. The first was when the British, for imperialistic reasons, decided that they must crush the Boer Republic by force of arms, first 'illegally' by the Jameson Raid of 1896 into the Transvaal and, three years later, 'legally' when the Boers declared war on Great Britain. After the Jameson Raid the Kaiser sent a telegram of congratulation to the Boer leader, Paul Kruger: during the Boer War, Germany was sympathetic to the Afrikaaners. These acts and attitudes were construed, by many Britons, as evidence of hostility.

Far more important than such diplomatic irritants was the new German naval strategy. Before the introduction of Admiral von Tirpitz's first Navy Bill, in 1898, there had been only a local, defensive fleet, a sort of coastguard, in the Baltic and the North Sea. This was all rapidly changed. The Kaiser, who had opened the Kiel Canal in 1895, thus giving the German navy free access from a safe Baltic port to the North Sea and hence the oceans of the world, remarked in his usual strident tone that Germany's future lay upon the blue water. With his army near to perfection – certainly there was no professional army of its size so well trained, well equipped and well led in the world of Kaiser Wilhelm II – he set about building a comparable navy, rapidly. By 1903 there were twenty-seven German battleships afloat. They were newer, better gunned and at least as well crewed as the sixty-seven then possessed by Britain. In 1906 more were ordered, both in Berlin and in London. But by then the concept of a two-fleet navy had become meaningless. Therefore, as early as 1903, the British had taken the first, tentative steps towards an alliance with France, the so-called *Entente Cordiale* with the old, hereditary enemy: and, through those steps, an inevitable implicit alliance with the newer enemy, Russia. The lines of power were thus laid out in Europe: Central Europe,

Cartoon from *Kladderadatsch*, 1909. Naval race between England and Germany.

Gesetzlich geschützt. N° 3407

Prinz Heinrich

German postcards. *Above*, German fleet, 1900. *Below*, Kiel Harbour, 1908.

Kiel, Kriegshafen.

Kaiser Wilhelm II and King Friedrich of Saxony, 18 October 1913, at the unveiling of a memorial on the centenary of the Battle of Leipzig.

from the Baltic to Sicily on the one hand, the great nations of East and West upon the other. In the two world wars to come, the tergiversation of Italy in both wars was, strategically, of only marginal importance, as was the great difference of opinion and of ideology between the Eastern and Western allies, for Kaiser Wilhelm II had succeeded in achieving precisely what Bismarck had struggled so long to avoid, the isolation of Germany. This was construed in Germany as a hostile 'encirclement'. A series of political crises, such as Agadir in 1911 and the several Balkan wars, in most of which the Kaiser indulged in considerable sabre-rattling, only served to increase successive British governments' distrust of German motives. Europe's power structure was set up, and was fought for, in a savage way that was to endure throughout at least half a century.

This system of alliances, the Triple Alliance of Germany, Austria and Italy, the Triple Entente of Russia, France and Britain, looked neat enough on paper, a true balance of power. In fact it was a house of cards. Italy was to fail her allies in 1915 and again in 1943, France did the same in 1940, as did Russia in 1917 and again in 1944, while Germany's involvement in the Balkan affairs of Austria's ramshackle empire was the direct cause of World War I, the destruction of the German Empire and of the painstaking values that had been built up throughout the Biedermeier and Bismarckian nineteenth century. It has been said that boredom was the prime motive in Europe's attempt at suicide, that the governing classes of the great European states, satiated with the slaughter of birds and animals, ceasing to find much satisfaction in religion, enjoying great financial and sexual freedom, wanted *something to happen*. Well, it did, in 1914, and through cheering crowds the young men of Europe marched off to their death.

An Italian general addressing troops before going into action in World War I.

August 1914. At the outbreak of World War I, crowds greet the German Crown Prince in Unter den Linden, Berlin.

Germany artillery troops pass through Brussels in 1914.

A German dugout is converted into French trenches after the capture of Fort Douaumont, 1916.

The German Great General Staff had based its war plans on a single front campaign in the West involving the invasion of neutral Belgium, if not also of Holland (the Schlieffen Plan). Ignoring Holland to their detriment, the Germans yet very nearly conquered France in a very few weeks before the British could honour, in strength, their Belgian commitment. For well over three years trench warfare, punctuated by useless mass attacks that won a few hundred yards at a vast cost in loss of life (the Germans alone lost some two million soldiers), ensued on the Western Front. In March 1918, with Russia knocked out of the war and in a state of revolution, the Germans launched a final, desperate offensive in the West which, with the assistance of un-restricted U-boat warfare, again nearly succeeded. However, the Americans were now in the war, and though the part their armies played in 1918 was comparatively insignificant, by 1919 they would have provided a very formidable force. In November 1918 the Germans surrendered, fighting bravely to the end, and the Kaiser abdicated in favour of a Republic. It was a surrender to exhaustion and anticipation rather than a straight military defeat. The Kaiser had undermined Bismarck's work: he left it in ruins.

The stupidity of these generally well-meaning politicians and diplomats who organized and implemented catastrophe was matched only by their ability to survive the destruction of the societies which they were supposed to protect. Only in the defeated countries, which in this context must include not only Germany and Austria, but also Russia and Italy, were the old leaders dispensed with, usually by violent revolutionary methods. Time scales, however, were different. In Germany, unlike in Russia, the civil servants who had administered the country while some millions of their compatriots perished or starved to death, continued at their desks. Even the second German revolution, the Nazi one, failed to dislodge the *Beamtentum* which, like a vastly multiplied Vicar of Bray, served Kaiser, Republic, Hitler, the Allied Occupation Forces and, once again, the truncated Federal Republic in the western, the Russians and their Communist nominees in the eastern part of the Germanies. If there are heirs to the Teutonic Knights, prepared to fight on any front and against any enemy in the ill-defined interest of their beliefs, then these are they, grey and unknown men, armed with more powerful, more modern weapons than the sword or the machine-gun, armed with typewriter and telephone.

*   *   *

The century between the Battle of Waterloo and the Battle of the Marne was marked by a steady and indeed accelerating German progress not only in industrial technology but in the pure sciences and their subsidiary fields. German medicine, for instance, attained a very high standard, in many respects probably the highest in the world. German agronomists, too, were very skilled and the yield of the farmers' acres rose almost year by year.

In the arts, however, it was a sadder tale, save only in music. Great composers continued to appear in Germany and Austria, with the finest orchestras and instrumentalists to play their own music and that of their great predecessors. Mendelssohn, Wagner, Brahms, Mahler, Richard Strauss, the roll-call is as glorious as it is impressive. At a more popular level the waltzes of the Viennese Johann Strauss, the operettas of Offenbach (who became a French national) and later of Hungarian-born Franz Lehar swept the world. In music, the most international of the arts, the artistic genius of the German-Austrian nineteenth and early twentieth centuries found its supreme expression. Germany and Italy were the two poles of European music, with of course constant cross-fertilization at every level, from great composers to second violinists. German music, yes even Wagner despite the Nazis' prostitution of his work, is the greatest monument to the German spirit of the age.

The other arts fared less well. There were competent German paint-ers and sculptors, needless to say, but to our eyes their work seems generally dull, particularly if one draws a highly invidious comparison with what the French then were doing before, during and after the great Impressionist outburst, even with what Constable and Turner were doing in England. A representative collection of the very best German art of the nineteenth century would appeal to few save his-torians. This was to change in the new century. The *Blaue Reiter* manifesto of the Munich Expressionists was published in 1912. The signatories included Franz Marc, the Russian Kandinsky, Feininger, Paul Klee, Macke and the Austrian composer Arnold Schoenberg, among others. By that time Expressionist poets had also published some of their earlier work. In fact quite a few members of this essen-tially German artistic movement were to lose their lives in World War I, including Marc himself, whose famous painting had given its name to the original manifesto. But German Expressionism did not really become a powerful force, with particularly spectacular schools of artists and writers in Berlin, Düsseldorf and elsewhere, until after

Justus von Liebig (1803–73). Chemist and agronomist (*left*).

Paul Ehrlich (1854–1915). Bacteriologist and joint winner of the Nobel Prize for medicine in 1908 (*right*).

DER
BLAUE
REITER

Horse in Landscape. Painting by Franz Marc, 1910.

World War I. Like Dadaism, entirely postwar in Germany, being a Swiss import, and its offspring, Surrealism, Expressionism was unpopular with the Nazis – despite or perhaps because its incidental artistic brutality foreshadowed the real brutality to come – and perished or at least went underground between 1933 and 1945 or later.

Literature, too, passed through a generally dull period after the death of Goethe in 1832. Not only Classicism but also Romanticism had become, or were on their way to become, a spent force. There are few German novelists or poets worth reading until the appearance, at the very end of the century or early in the new, of such men as Thomas Mann, Rainer Maria Rilke, Stefan George, and these, too, really ushered in the new age. The one startling exception is the poet and philosopher Friedrich Nietzsche (1844–1900), a veritable comet who brilliantly illuminated the German skies before he sank down into madness. He truly hated the spirit of the age, its religiosity, its nationalism,

Design for cover of *Der Blaue Reiter* almanac by Wassily Kandinsky, 1911–12 (*left*).

its liberalism and indeed its whole basic philosophy. Many have maintained that he was the spiritual grandfather of Nazism, though certainly Hitler could not have understood – if he ever tried to read other than quote the titles of – Nietzsche's quasi-anarchical despair, and it is equally certain that had he lived, in his right mind, to the age of one hundred Nietzsche would have despised the Nazis, their motives and their methods. Nevertheless there is something very sinister in Nietzsche's magnificent writing, for at the very highest intellectual level it becomes at last an appeal to the primeval forest, a lust for the pre-Christian world.

If imaginative writing of the highest order, both in poetry and prose, was sadly lacking during most of this period, what might be described as the conjoint arts, philosophy, economics and history, flourished, though with an ever growing academic flavour. Arthur Schopenhauer (1788–1860) had published *World as Will and Idea* in 1819, but went on developing his wise if pessimistic thoughts. As late as 1870 Wagner's *Essay on Beethoven* was a study of the metaphysics of music in terms of Schopenhauer's philosophy. And then there was Karl Marx. At the end of the period Oswald Spengler (1880–1936) was

Friedrich Nietzsche (1844–1900).

Illustration from *Jugend*, 1906. Nietzsche-inspired 'Superman and Mate', by Fidus.

working on his *Decline of the West*, although this monumental work of anthropology, sociology, history and philosophy, as pessimistic in its own way as was Schopenhauer's in his – and as its title implies – was not published until 1918. As for the more normal type of historians, they raised German historiography to a par with the greatest scholarship of Europe. It is only necessary to name Leopold von Ranke (1795–1886) and Theodor Mommsen (1817–1903) to make this point: and there were many others, based largely upon the great German universities which rightly enjoyed a fame equivalent to that of Oxford or Cambridge, Harvard or Yale, the Sorbonne or Rome.

Finally one phenomenon of the period which must be touched upon was the massive emigration of Germans to the United States of America, so that for a time parts of the American continent, and particularly the Middle West, seemed to be almost an extension of the Reich, a Germany *outre-mer*, until these new Americans became assimilated in their new country, a process virtually completed by the time American declared war on Germany in 1917.

In view of Germany's high and growing prosperity this flight of millions seems odd at first glance. However, there were at least three

Arthur Schopenhauer (1788–1860). Painting by Justus Lunteschütz, *c.* 1850 (*above*).

The historian Theodor Mommsen (1817–1903) talking with the sculptor Reinhold Begas.

good reasons for it. After the crushing of the 1848 Revolution, and the imposition of a reactionary government, many liberals preferred to emigrate. They found freedom in the New World, they prospered, and others followed. Secondly the steady rationalization of German agriculture meant the dispossession, by economic or other means, of many peasant-proprietors and farm labourers. Many of these did not wish to become industrial workers and followed the liberal middle-class emigrés to plough and sow in the Dakotas and elsewhere. They too prospered, and wrote home, and were followed across the seas by friends and relatives. And thirdly there were those who found the stuffy, socially stratified and militarily dominated atmosphere of Prussia and Imperial Germany unattractive. They were ambitious: they wanted fresh air: and the blood that they had inherited from their nomadic ancestors drove them across the ocean, where they became, quite rapidly, good and patriotic Americans.

Cartoon from *Simplicissimus*, 1897, 'Bemonocled lieutenant setting the style even in a Turkish bath'.

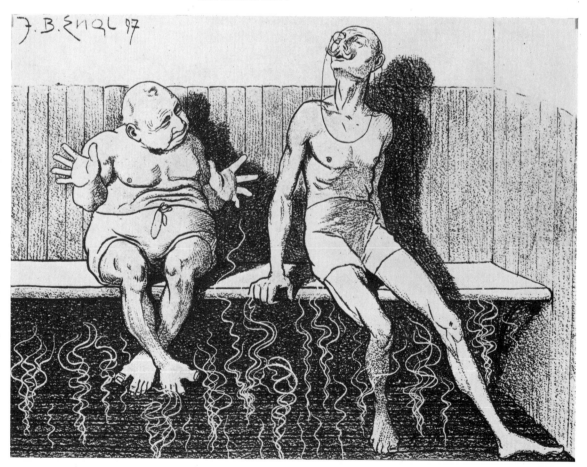

CHAPTER TEN

The Weimar Republic
1918–1933

The rather *simpliste* polarization of European politics into 'left' and 'right' that followed the German and Russian revolutions of 1917–19 and culminated in the Spanish Civil War of 1936–39 has implied, and in the eyes of most historians has continued to imply, the very greatest significance to the year 1933. The period between 1918 and that date is referred to as the 'Weimar Period', the next twelve years as the 'Nazi period'. Of course 1933 was a great divide, but to pretend that a good, democratic Germany was instantly transformed into a horrible, totalitarian Nazi state is another gross oversimplification.

The Weimar Republic – so called because its constitution was promulgated in the town for ever associated with Goethe and the Enlightenment, and soon to achieve another fame when the Nazis built the concentration camp of Buchenwald in the beautiful beech forest where Goethe used to walk and meditate – was seldom a happy or even a successful formula for governing Germany. Born of despair, rent by five years of attempted civil war by Communists, monarchists and Nazis, by smothered frontier warfare with the French in the west and the Poles in the east, and by the worst inflation that Europe has ever seen, the Weimar Republic enjoyed half a decade of comparative peace and prosperity in the late 1920s before going down in a miserable welter of unemployment (reaching some 30 per cent) and political ineptitude that followed on the world economic crisis. America had largely financed Germany during those few, good years. When America went broke, Germany went broker, and decided that democracy, American or British or French style, was a rotten way to run a country. To the general and growing acclaim of the majority of Germans, the Nazis took over.

Cartoon from *Simplicissimus*, 1919.
Versailles.

Poster by Käthe Kollwitz, 1923.
'German children are starving'
(*below*).

Friedrich Ebert, the first president of Germany, proclaims the German Constitution, July 1919.

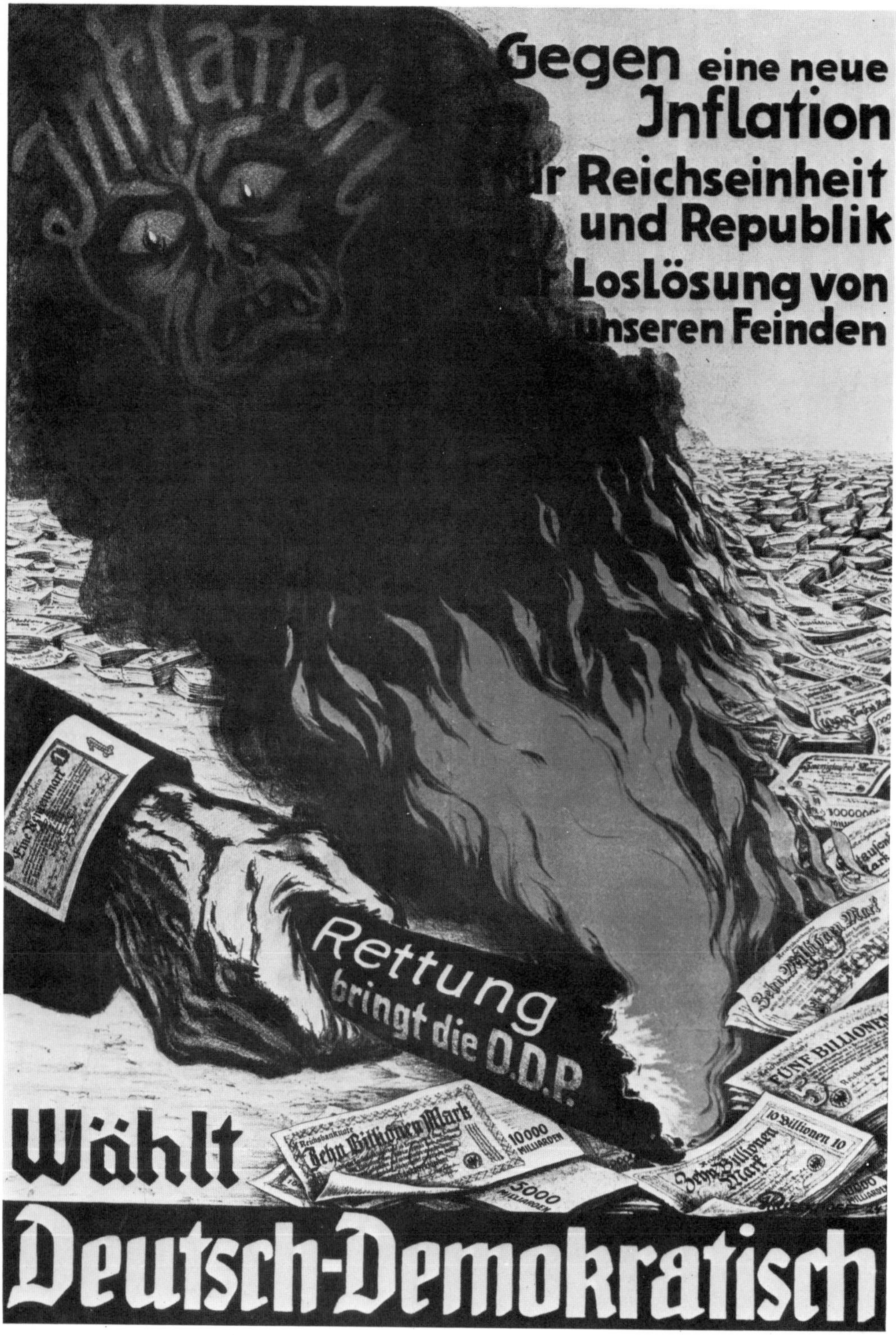

Inflation
Gegen eine neue
Inflation
ür Reichseinheit
und Republik
Loslösung von
unseren Feinden
Rettung
bringt die D.D.P.
FÜNF BILLIONEN
Wählt
Deutsch-Demokratisch

Cartoon from *Simplicissimus*, 14 May 1923, at the height of inflation. Gustav Stresemann, then Prime Minister, with caption 'He looks left, he looks right – he will save me.'

The significance of Weimar was not temporal – a mere five or six years are of little importance in the history of a great nation. It had however the greatest meaning in two ways that would seem to be directly opposed. On the one hand this was the loose political soil into which the totalitarian ideologies, Communism and Nazism, could strike deep roots. On the other it did, in its inefficient fashion, set a democratic precedent, hitherto unknown in Germany, which was to be of the greatest value to Konrad Adenauer and his successors in the government of the Federal Republic after 1949. This dual heritage takes concrete shape in the present physical division of Germany into two states, indeed in the Berlin Wall itself, which physically delineates the moral and political frontier between totalitarian tyranny and parliamentary democracy.

Weimar's early years were not only marked by extreme internal turbulence. It was during this period that the German army, the

Election poster produced by the German Democratic Party, 1924 (*left*).

Willst Du dies?

Vereinigung zur Bekämpfung
des Bolschewismus
Berlin W.9, Schellingstr. 2

Paul Helwig
19

German anti-Bolshevik poster, 1919.
'Is this what you want?'

Reichswehr, assumed a new and curious role. The soldiers who had
fought on the Western and Southern Fronts marched back from
defeat, bands playing and flags flying, and it was not hard to persuade
the general public, and soon enough many of the soldiers themselves,
that they were 'undefeated in the field', that they had been 'stabbed in
the back' by revolutionaries at home. Some of the units on the Eastern
Front had, it is true, been infected with revolutionary, Communist
ideology, but in general the army was anti-revolutionary and set about
with energy crushing revolutionary movements in various parts of
Germany. (Parts of Bavaria, including Munich, formed at one time
and briefly a Soviet republic: parts of Berlin were solidly red: while
bands of marauders, who called themselves Communists, roamed the
countryside more, it would seem, in search of loot than of the Marxist
Utopia.) Against these people the army reacted strongly and with
toughness, and by the end of 1919 the possibility of a Communist
(Spartacist) takeover in Germany, on which Lenin and his colleagues
had in large measure relied, had receded. In March of the following

year an attempt at a militarist takeover, the so-called *Kapp Putsch*, also failed. General von Lüttwitz, Commandant of Berlin, forced the government to flee the capital, but though the *Reichswehr* did not fight him and his followers, no more did it give him the backing he needed and expected. It stood aloof, and the *Kapp Putsch* foundered on the solid opposition of the Socialists and trade unionists in a general strike. Finally when Hitler attempted to seize power in Munich in 1923, backed by General Erich Ludendorff, one of Germany's great war heroes, the army was once again hostile to these new-style revolutionaries.

The position of the army in German public life between the Treaty of Versailles (1919) and the outbreak of World War II in 1939 was peculiar, and derived very largely from the attitudes of the organizer of the post-war *Reichswehr*, General Hans von Seeckt, a most remarkable man, known as 'the Sphinx', though it must be said that he had comparatively little difficulty in imposing his views on his fellow officers,

Anti-Nazi cartoon from *Simplicissimus*, 1923.

for these they usually shared already. The German officer corps did not like the new Republic, and indeed they had an icy contempt for politicians as such: they had sworn their oath of loyalty to the Kaiser, and he was in exile in Holland. However, Seeckt was quite shrewd enough to realize, particularly during and after the *Kapp Putsch*, that any attempt at a restoration of the monarchy or even at a military *coup d'etat* was bound to fail in the climate of post-war Germany and would only discredit the army. This he was at all costs determined to avoid, and he was able to use the terms of the Versailles Treaty – by which the German forces were limited in theory to an army of 100,000 men without tanks, with a token navy deprived of U-boats and no air force – for his own purposes. This small army he and his staff officers (the Great German General Staff had also been disbanded by the Treaty, but continued to function under a cover name) trained to the highest possible degree of efficiency, so that it became an 'army of N.C.O.s' prepared for the day of expansion when virtually every private could become a sergeant platoon commander overnight and every second lieutenant a major in command of a battalion. This, indeed, was to happen. With such a strong militarist tradition, inherited from Imperial Germany, from Prussia and from the Teutonic Knights themselves, Seeckt had little difficulty in collecting the very cream of Germany's manpower into his small army, which he then moulded into a tight instrument entirely obedient to his General Staff. Amid the shifting storm clouds of German politics, Seeckt's *Reichswehr* seemed a veritable lion of bronze, patriotic, incorruptible and above the struggle as no conscript army in a democracy can ever be.

In fact Seeckt, his fellow generals and his successors were far more involved in politics than they allowed the public to see. ('Be more than you appear to be' remained their basic intention.) They were determined to get around, and eventually destroy, the Treaty of Versailles. When the inflation ended, late in 1923, and Field-Marshal von Hindenburg was elected president in 1925 in succession to the Socialist Ebert who bore the opprobrium of the 1918 surrender, the army felt that it had the next best man to a Kaiser as head of state. What had been a purely tactical support of the German Republic thus became tinged with an element of emotional support as well. Hindenburg, perhaps above all other Germans, was one of their own. He seems to have regarded his presidency as a caretaker appointment against the day when the Hohenzollerns, whom the old soldier had served so loyally, so successfully and for so long, should come into their own again. And he listened to his generals.

They had already exerted considerable pressure upon his predecessor, Ebert, and his governments, and this for two reasons, both connected with Germany's determination to flout the Treaty of

Versailles. It was a punitive treaty. Apart from an attempt to disarm Germany permanently, it also tried to extract massive reparations from the conquered and partly occupied country. There were very few Germans who did not hate the Treaty of Versailles. Even after the German surrender the British continued the economic blockade, causing the death through starvation of a great many civilians. The French, in their determination to extract reparations, occupied the Ruhr and encouraged a separatist movement in the Rhineland. The Germans fought the French in the streets for a little while, but made the whole Ruhr operation economically pointless by allowing inflation to render the mark valueless. Seeckt brought great political pressure to bear on the Social-Democrat coalition governments. The two pariahs of Europe, Germany and Russia, should draw together, he said. In the mid-Weimar period, this appealed to the Socialists, for political reasons, and to the Nationalists, since it offered a way out of the confines of Versailles. For the army it meant that they could, in exchange for technological knowledge, use Russia as a country in which to try out the weapons they were forbidden to have in Germany and there to train some of their troops in the use of tanks and military

President Ebert, Chancellor Wirth and General von Seeckt taking the salute of the Reichswehr, 11 August 1922.

127

Amtliche Nachricht der Preußischen Staatsregierung.

Zusammenbruch der Militärdiktatur!

Mit dem heutigen Tage ist die Militärherrschaft, die eine kleine Schar in Berlin aufzurichten versucht hat, zusammengebrochen. Kapp und General von Lüttwitz sind von ihren angemaßten Ämtern zurückgetreten. Den Oberbefehl über die in Berlin stationierten Truppen hat auf Anordnung der Reichsregierung der General v. Seeckt übernommen. Die Sicherung der Reichshauptstadt übernehmen die der Regierung treugebliebenen Bestandteile der Sicherheitswehr und der bereits früher in Berlin einquartierten Reichswehr. Die unter General von Lüttwitz einmarschierten Truppen werden schleunigst und zwar spätestens bis Donnerstag Abend aus Berlin herausgeführt. Alle Zeitungsbesetzungen, Telephonzensur und die sonstigen von der Militärdiktatur angeordneten Maßnahmen werden sofort aufgehoben.

An der einmütigen entschiedenen Abwehr von Arbeiterschaft und Bürgertum ist die Militärdiktatur zerschellt.

Unser Volk wird die neu erkämpfte Freiheit für alle Zeit zu wahren wissen.

Berlin, den 17. März 1920.

Die Preußische Staatsregierung.
gez. Hirsch.

Poster announcing the collapse of the *Kapp Putsch*, 17 March 1920.

aircraft. Much as the German generals disliked Communism, much as the Kremlin feared and distrusted German militarism, each was prepared to use the other quite cynically. Apart from the Russo-German cold war during the early years of the Hitler government, to be dramatically ended by the Hitler-Stalin Pact of August 1939, German-Russian friendship, at the military and in some measure at the political level, endured for some twenty years, until at last the German army invaded Russia in June 1941.

Nor was that the only way in which the German General Staff was politically active behind the scenes. More than once a representative of the Army High Command, a Seeckt or later General von Schleicher perhaps, would deliver the acid comment to the president: 'the army no longer has confidence in the present government of the Reich'. Then and speedily that government would be sent packing. That army has been frequently described as 'a state within the state'. This is not quite true, but certainly it was a very powerful element within the state, with its allegiance principally to itself, and utterly remote from democratic methods. It was equally remote from Hitler's methods. When, in June 1934, Hitler's SS (*Schutzstaffel*), his personal bodyguard, murdered the leaders of Hitler's SA (*Sturmabteilungen*), the brown-shirted street fighters, and indeed some of the army's own people, the army did not soil their kid gloves by intervening. As at the time of the *Kapp Putsch* they stood back and watched with a measure of contempt while the gangsters destroyed one another. They did not apparently realize that by so doing they were in effect signing their own death-warrants though their execution was to be postponed for a little over ten years.

Adolf Hitler at a Nuremberg rally, 1923, *left*, and *right*, 'Germany awake!' Banner carried in a Bavarian Nationalist procession, 1923.

Election poster, 1931. 'Vote National Socialist!'

Although Nazism suffered an almost complete eclipse for some seven years after the failure of Hitler's 'Beer Hall *Putsch*' in 1923 much that had happened during that period was, quite unconsciously, preparing the way for the tyranny to come.

The inflation, by wiping out savings, had pauperized large elements of the middle and particularly of the lower middle classes. These poor people had no wish to become members of the proletariat, nor did they want to throw in their lot politically with the great working-class parties, the Social Democrats or the Communists. On the other hand they felt that they had somehow been swindled by the Weimar 'system' and though they continued for the time being to vote for right-wing, conservative parties or, if Catholics, for the so-called Centre Party, they were patently disaffected, even alienated, from the democratic process which they already regarded as something that had been thrust upon them, in defeat, by their enemies. Furthermore, not everyone had suffered in the inflation. Clever, often unscrupulous, men had as usual made fortunes out of the misery of others. The flamboyance of these *nouveaux riches* only served further to embitter the minor civil servant or small shopkeeper who had seen his life's savings wiped out in a matter of weeks. With the economic collapse of the early 1930s these people flocked to Hitler and indeed provided the backbone of the Nazi (German National Socialist Workers') Party.

Wilhelm Busch, artist, and Herrmann Levi, conductor, 'Christian and Jew under one roof'. pre-1914.

While in Landsberg Prison, in 1924, Hitler dictated his book, *Mein Kampf*, to Rudolf Hess. It is at first glance a curious fact that the two most seminally important political books of the past hundred years, Hitler's and Karl Marx's *Das Kapital*, should both be written in so turgid a style as to render them almost unreadable. Indeed few people ever did read *Mein Kampf*, yet the message, oversimplified, got across. It was that Hitler intended to re-create a great and powerful Germany, to include all the German people: this new state would need 'living room' which was to be found in the Slav lands to the east, perhaps by diplomacy, more probably by force. Meanwhile all Germany's present miseries were ascribed to the Jews. It was the Jews who had 'betrayed' the German army in 1918. It was Russian Jews who controlled the German Communist Party. It was Western Jews, particularly the Jews of Wall Street, who had caused the inflation. And it was German Jews who had profited from all these national catastrophes. 'The Jews are our misfortune', Hitler and the Nazis proclaimed again and again and again.

Wilhelmine Germany had never been particularly anti-semitic, less so certainly than pre-1914 France or Russia, less so than the United States, comparable to Edwardian England in this respect, for the German Jews were as patriotic as the English Jews, anxious to be assimilated and not at all international in their outlook. On the other

Walther Rathenau leaving the
Foreign Office in Berlin, 1922.

hand anti-semitism was rife in Austria and particularly in Vienna, and it was in that city that Hitler had spent his early years and imbibed the disgusting doctrine.

Three factors made Germany fertile for the poison that Hitler imported from Vienna. The new state of Poland, re-created by the Versailles Treaty, was ruthlessly anti-semitic, and many Polish Jews emigrated. Most of these went to Britain or to the United States, but some and usually the poorest sought refuge from their Polish perse-cutors in democratic Germany. It is one of many paradoxes that the anti-semitism of the Poles was in some measure historical hatred of the Germans. The Jews from Germany had, in the Middle Ages, followed the German conquerors of the Poles, speaking a form of German called Yiddish. During World War I General Luden-dorff, soon enough to become briefly a Nazi, had even issued a pam-phlet, in Yiddish, reminding the Polish Jews of their German-based ancestry. Yet they were not welcome *revenants*. Speaking a weird mish-mash of German, Polish and Yiddish, strangely dressed, with long ringlets, they were obviously foreigners. It was not hard for the Nazi propagandists to extrapolate the exotic appearance of the Polish Jews, first, by grossly exaggerating their number and, secondly, by stating that *all* Jews were foreigners, including former German-Jewish officers of World War I and even highly patriotic cabinet ministers such as Walther Rathenau who had most brilliantly organ-ized Germany's war economy and, for his pains, was murdered by extreme nationalists while Nazism was still in its infancy.

Secondly, a few of the revolutionaries of 1918 were indeed Jewish. It was not hard to say that they all were. Some of the war and inflation profiteers were Jewish. Again, by concentrating on this element, blame for all profiteering could be ascribed to all Jews.

Thirdly, the Jews, being a clever and industrious people, had done well in the professions in which they were acceptable, particularly in the press, medicine and the law. Here it was easy for the Nazi propa-ganda machine to appeal to non-Jewish envy, to maintain that in their clannish way the Jewish doctors, lawyers and journalists were corner-ing the professions and the media for their own people. That this was palpably untrue did not deter the Nazis, who believed in the big lie.

Finally, always and everywhere in times of misery, and nowhere more so than in Germany, a scapegoat is needed. Surely, the Germans said, good Germans could not be responsible for the miseries of the time? There must be a deep-rooted conspiracy. But who were the conspirators? Hitler provided the answer, without so much as a shred of evidence to support his monstrous lies. Many Germans were dis-gusted by Hitler's and Goebbels' anti-semitic propaganda, but many more were not.

A Jew in the midst of a group of
German policemen, *c.* 1933 (*right*).

Industry. Painting by Schulze-Sölde.

Still from Fritz Lang's film, *Metropolis*, 1925.

Once Dr Hjalmar Schacht, the president of the Reichsbank, had stabilized the mark in late 1923, German industry and commerce rapidly recovered. Despite massive confiscations, in the form both of goods and of money, by the victorious allies, by 1927 Germany was as powerful economically and its G.N.P. in almost all respects as great as it had been in 1913. However, there had been a socio-economic shift, for which the most convenient word is 'cartelization'. Many small businesses had gone to the wall, under the pressures of war and inflation. The bigger ones survived and rapidly grew bigger yet as they swallowed their smaller rivals. Huge industrial combines dominated the German economy, controlling every stage of production, from basic raw materials to commercial outlets. There were thus comparatively few offices that the Nazis needed to control in order to acquire domination over the most important sectors of the German economy such as heavy industry, chemicals and electrical plants. In the early 1930s, before ever the Nazis obtained office, many big industrialists such as Krupp, Stinnes or Flesch, frightened by the growing strength of the German Communist Party that matched the weakening of will of successive 'Weimar' governments, were not only prepared to play ball with the Nazis but in many cases to finance them.

Berlin-Brietz. Housing for workers in the Weimar period.

Weimar Germany was never so far advanced a 'welfare state' as was Socialist Austria at that time, where it is said that every newborn baby was supplied with a free ticket to the crematorium. However, the health and other benefits instigated by Bismarck were extended far beyond what then prevailed in Britain, France or the United States. This meant that the citizen was increasingly dependent upon the State, whose powers were thus extended and could be used for any purpose that the government saw fit. Paternalism, ever strong in German family life, assumed in political terms ever greater *étatisme*. When the State failed to carry out its fatherly duties, as it appeared to be doing during the Depression, then it was time to find a new father. Hitler was ready to oblige.

Much, probably too much, has been made of the financial and above all of the sexual immorality of Weimar Germany. To the present-day inhabitants of London or New York, Berlin in the 1920s would hardly come as a surprise. To the German middle class of the period, however, the open flaunting of homosexuality, the multitude of prostitutes, the availability of pornography and the general decline of the bourgeois virtues were both shocking and disgusting. They saw decadence all around them, and yearned for a restoration of Prussian discipline in this as in other fields. And Hitler promised them that, too.

National Socialist poster of 1933. 'Hitler – our last hope.'

Programme for *Schall und Rauch*, a cabaret, drawing by George Grosz (1893–1959).

But the greatest promise of all, as the figures of those out of work rose and rose again from 1930 to 1932, was that he could solve the unemployment problem. Well, the democratic politicians had failed: even the army had failed when it had so far departed from its traditions of aloofness as to allow General von Schleicher to serve as chancellor: why not see what Hitler could do? And on 30 January 1933, despite some loss of Nazi strength in the election of the previous November, President von Hindenburg appointed Adolf Hitler Chancellor of Germany, to head a right-wing coalition government. Within six months Hitler had dispensed with almost all the allies thrust upon him, had thrown his militant opponents into concentration camps, had dissolved all political parties save his own, and – apart from the army, which had again withdrawn from the political turmoil – was omnipotent in Germany.

The two friends, painted wood, by Ernst Kirchner, 1925–26 (*left*).

Collage by John Heartfield, *c.* 1932. Placard reads 'Any job taken' (*right*).

Cartoon from *Kladderadatsch*, 13 February 1933. Hindenburg blesses the union of Hitler and Stahlhelm's 'Old Soldier' party – based on Wagner's *Meistersinger*, Scene III.

CHAPTER ELEVEN

Hitler's Germany and World War II

Hitler's rapid rise to absolute power, first in Germany and, briefly, in almost all Europe, was based on two very sound tactical principles: divide and rule; and, destroy your enemies one by one. The first principle was effected administratively by an expensive duplication of functions at almost all levels between the Nazi Party apparatus and the Civil Service, including the police and the armed forces, that he had inherited from his predecessors. Furthermore, government was strictly compartmentalized. After the first months the cabinet never met, thus obviating the concept of 'cabinet responsibility', and in theory each minister was supposed to occupy himself solely with the affairs of his own department: only the police, soon headed by Heinrich Himmler, commander of Hitler's bodyguard, the SS, was perforce involved in all aspects of German life, for Germany became a police state which deliberately used terror to prevent any form of opposition. Only the army enjoyed a considerable measure of immunity from the *Gestapo* (the Secret State Police), and the other branches of the police force, but in exchange the army had to withdraw absolutely from politics. The generals were also bribed, on occasion quite blatantly with cash, but usually in a more subtle fashion, for they were given conscription (1935) and all the new weapons that they wanted, as Hitler demolished the terms of Versailles. For a decade Hitler treated his generals, and the army as a whole, with great respect. This they repaid by abstaining from politics and, when war came, by winning a series of great and spectacular victories.

The Reichstag Fire, for which the Nazi Party storm troopers, the SA, may or may not have been responsible in February 1933, was used as a pretext to declare the Communist Party an illegal organization, to

The Reichstag fire, February 1933.

give many SA men temporary police powers, and to round up the Communist leaders, many of their followers, as well as strong elements of the Social Democrat Party and of the trade union movement. Many Jews were simultaneously arrested. These men, and some women, were usually beaten up or tortured before being interned without trial in the concentration camps that Hermann Goering, a fighter ace of World War I, was busily setting up in various parts of Germany. All militant opposition on the Left having thus been emasculated, elections were held, and since many of the new Reichstag's deputies were behind barbed wire, Hitler obtained an absolute majority there (which he had not won in votes) for his Enabling Act, which gave him virtually unlimited dictatorial power, in March 1933. In August of the following year President von Hindenburg died, and Hitler announced his own appointment as president for life. This was a formality that made his total power legal as well as real. More important, he exacted a personal oath of loyalty to himself from the soldiers, an oath not to the head of state, as heretofore both during the Imperial and Weimar periods, but to the *Führer*, Adolf Hitler. By then the pattern of Nazi Germany had been firmly set: for his enemies, the terror of the concentration camps or death or both: from the rest of the German populace, total obedience.

Day of National Labour, 1 May 1933. President Hindenburg and Chancellor Hitler ride together to the festivities.

In the early days of his régime Hitler had relied in some measure upon the industrialists and on their political representatives, the German National Party. These watched, with approval, while the Left was brutally and physically destroyed. Their turn was soon to come. The German National Party was ignored in, and soon enough expelled from, government and wound up. There was only room for one political party in Hitler's monolithic state. Capitalism continued, but in ever greater measure German industry took its orders from the Nazi government. With the great upswing in rearmament, which rapidly soaked up much and eventually all unemployment, the industrialists had little to complain of, nor did they, and the steady liquidation of Jewish businesses was acceptable to many of their non-Jewish competitors, who profited therefrom.

This alliance, no matter how temporary and how loaded in the Nazis' favour, was not popular with certain elements within the National Socialist Party itself, for many of its members, particularly among the street fighters of the SA, took the 'socialist' element in its name seriously. True, Hitler had eliminated many of his Socialist extremists before he ever came to power, but by early 1934 he had reason to distrust the SA as such, principally because it was too powerful. Its leader was a homosexual bravo named Ernst Roehm, the only man who was allowed to address the leader in the intimate second person singular. An utterly devoted Nazi, he had one personal ambition: to control the German army and eventually to incorporate it into his own vast, irregular, ill-trained and largely Socialist private army. Such an idea was of course repulsive to the German officer corps. Hitler pondered, and then made a deal with the German generals. With their approval, but without their active participation – for he used Heinrich Himmler's SS – he destroyed the leadership of the SA by a sudden act of mass murder in June 1934. He personally arrested his old friend Roehm, though too squeamish to shoot him with his own hand, as Roehm requested. He also took the opportunity to eliminate other enemies, including the army's own General von Schleicher. After the 'Night of the Long Knives' the SA ceased to have any political or military importance. Their brown shirts were still to be seen in the streets but the black-uniformed SS became the Party's military force, a role that they were to fulfil with ever-growing power and strength until the very end of the régime. Meanwhile the German public, sickened by the excesses of the SA, was not displeased to see them crushed. The public hoped that life might now return to normal, and Hitler encouraged them in this belief. The period between the summer of 1934 and early 1938 was one of comparative tranquillity, at least by Nazi standards. And when the foreigners poured into Berlin for the Olympic Games of 1936 they reported

Members of the Hitler Youth
Movement at a Nazi Congress
in Nuremberg, 1936.

home that all was quiet in Germany. They did not of course visit the
concentration camps, through which it has been estimated that some
six million Jews and other 'enemies of the Party' passed, and in which
many died or languished in misery, during the period between 1933
and the end of World War II.

Officially Nazi policy during the early, pre-war period was summed
up in the almost untranslatable word *Gleichschaltung*, which might be
rendered as 'the imposition of parity'. This vaguely socialistic, muddy
concept was applied in numerous ways and in numerous fields.
Although the various German monarchies, such as Bavaria and
Saxony, had been abolished in 1918, Weimar had allowed the
territories to maintain a measure of internal sovereignty. This was now

Nazi poster, 1937.
'The Eternal Jew'.

abolished, and all power was vested in the central government. At
another level all organizations, even such harmless and apolitical ones
as Boy Scouts or amateur fishing clubs, were compelled to merge into
the equivalent National Socialist bodies, such as the Hitler Youth,
and the Nazi Labour Front took over all trade unions, which it
proceeded to dissolve. In fact *Gleichschaltung* was an obscure word for
the total Nazification of all Germany, at every level.

Hand in hand with this went the mounting pressure of anti-semitic
legislation. German Jews were gradually expelled from the professions,
and soon enough forbidden to sit on park benches. The Nuremberg
Laws were promulgated in the very early years of the Nazi régime,
mean and spiteful legislation which forbade non-Jewish servants to

147

The gates of Auschwitz
concentration camp, inscribed 'Work
makes free'.

'The burning of the books',
perpetrated by Dr Goebbels. Collage
by John Heartfield (*right*).

serve Jews among other such matters. In November 1938, on Nazi
orders, a *pogrom* was carried out, the synagogues burned, Jewish
shops wrecked, and many Jews thrown into the camps. All remaining
Jews who could left Germany, particularly men of any prominence.
Those remaining, men, women and children, were mostly deported
to extermination camps in the East, Auschwitz, Maidanek and elsewhere, they were put to death together with millions of other non-
German Jews.

How much did the Germans know of the atrocities being committed by their government? The answer is that they knew enough.
For example, everyone was aware that the concentration camps existed
and the people incarcerated in them treated with brutality, but
the details were generally unknown: former inmates were forbidden
to speak of their experiences under threat of re-arrest. The torments
inflicted upon their fellow citizens of Jewish or half-Jewish or even
quarter-Jewish blood were visible to all. And of course *Gleichschaltung*
affected almost everybody both in his or her public and private life.

Yet almost all Germans accepted this. The only way public opinion could express itself was through periodic plebiscites. The polls in favour of the government were, as it seemed at the time, almost incredibly favourable, 97, 98 or 99 per cent '*Ja!*' We now know that these figures were not in fact faked. The German nation was overwhelmingly grateful to Hitler for having solved the unemployment problem, for having imposed an apparent social order, and for making their country strong, great and for a decade extremely successful in international affairs, first in the diplomatic and then in the military fields. A few may have regretted the destruction of the arts ('decadent' according to Goebbels), literature, causing even non-Jewish intellectuals such as Thomas Mann and Stefan George to prefer exile: a few more the damage caused to the sciences, when great Jews such as Einstein and Freud were driven abroad from Germany and later from Austria: they can scarcely have amounted to the 1, 2 or 3 per cent who voted '*Nein!*' in the plebiscites. Germany, with its

Detail of a mural by Ben Shahn, 1937–38, showing Einstein and other refugees arriving in the U.S.A.

expanding army, air force and navy, with its new *Autobahns*, with its smoking factory chimneys, with its internal critics out of sight in Dachau or Oranienburg, in Buchenwald or in Belsen, was like an enormously powerful car driving at full throttle down one of the new military super-highways that Hitler built. And Hitler was indisputably at the wheel. It was, for the Germans, an exhilarating experience after what they regarded as years of frustrating stagnation.

This sense of purpose even spread to Germans beyond the borders of the Reich. True, an attempted Nazi takeover in Vienna, which involved the murder of Dr Engelbert Dollfuss, the Austrian chancellor, in 1934 failed, but an ever growing Austrian Nazi Party remained. And in the following year the German inhabitants of the Saar voted, in entirely free elections, for reunification with the Fatherland. Hitler's next objective was the incorporation of all Germans into the Nazi state, but until his new *Wehrmacht* or Armed Forces were ready or at least formidable, he held his hand or played his cards with some care.

In 1936 he ordered his troops to reoccupy the demilitarized Rhineland. This was in contravention of the terms of the Treaty of Versailles,

Albert Einstein (1879–1955) as a young man *left*, and *right*, Thomas Mann (1875–1955). Painting by Wolf Ritz.

German troops reoccupy the Rhineland, 1936.

but by then almost everyone and not only in Germany regarded that treaty, which the Germans called a *Diktat*, as a dead letter. More important, it was a violation of the Treaty of Locarno, freely entered into by Gustav Stresemann, then minister for foreign affairs, in 1925. The French dithered, but did nothing, in part held back by the British who had themselves abrogated Versailles by signing a naval agreement with Germany in the previous year. Hitler was beginning to feel that he had the Western democracies on the defensive. And the Russian purges, which almost destroyed the Red Army General Staff, led him to believe that he had little to fear on that flank.

With the outbreak of the Spanish Civil War, though the Germans signed the Non-intervention Agreement, Hitler saw an excellent opportunity to train his new armed forces, particularly the air force and elements of armoured (*Panzer*) divisions, in combat conditions. He did so, and they contributed – far more than the large Italian forces committed in Spain – to General Franco's victory over the Republicans.

In 1938 he decided that the time had come to take over Austria, once again as in the case of the Rhineland against the advice of his generals whom he overruled. (The more conservative generals, such as Blomberg and Fritsch, he had already fired, on trumped-up sexual charges such as he had used to justify the murder of Roehm.) Apart from a certain wringing of hands, the Western powers did nothing, and by now Hitler had forged an alliance with his Italian counterpart, Mussolini, who had been prepared to defend Austria in 1934, but was no longer willing to do so.

Hitler immediately turned his basilisk eye on Czechoslovakia, now also outflanked in the south, and which was in a state of latent hostility to Poland in the north (a country with which Hitler had signed an alliance in 1935) and to Hungary in the south-east, a country reliant on Italian support. There was a large German population in the frontier district, the Sudetenland, allegedly ill-treated by the Czechs and anxious to be united with the new, powerful Germany. In Munich, on 29 September 1938, the British and French, ill-prepared for war, surrendered the Sudetenland in defiance of the Franco-Czech treaty of alliance. In March 1939 Hitler occupied the whole of Czecho-

The Munich Peace Conference, October 1938. Chamberlain, Daladier, Hitler, Mussolini and Ciano.

The *Duce* and the *Führer*.
Guarantors of Peace.

slovakia, while the Western Powers again wrung their hands. They
did not, however, do nothing, for the British at least began to strengthen their defences, most particularly their air force, and to create
Eastern European alliances, with Poland and Rumania, while
Hitler's gaze became fixed upon the large German-speaking population of western Poland, Danzig and the so-called Polish Corridor
that gave Poland an outlet to the sea between East Prussia and the
rest of Germany. Poland was now outflanked, even as Czechoslovakia
had been. When Hitler performed a most surprising diplomatic
somersault by signing a treaty with Stalin on 25 August 1939, with a
secret clause stipulating another partition, Poland's doom was
certain, with or without British or French support. When a week later
the German army invaded Poland, the British and French declared
war. This seems to have taken Hitler by surprise, for he had expected
those countries once again to back down. World War II had started,
but with a total absence of enthusiasm, as compared to 1914, not only

in London and Paris but also in Berlin. Full employment and *Auto-bahns* yes, bloodless occupation of the Saar, the Rhineland, Austria and Czechoslovakia yes, a splendid new army and air force that had shown its mettle in Spain yes, even *Gleichschaltung* and concentration camps yes, but war was another matter. To Hitler's intense annoyance the crowds on the Unter den Linden did not cheer the *Panzer* division that paraded through Berlin on its way to the Polish front. Glumly the army's reservists kissed their wives or sweethearts goodbye and dutifully rejoined their units. Even the intelligent, informed staff officers did not believe that their country could win the war into which Hitler had launched them. Yet they went off, to do their duty as German patriots, and this they did extremely well and for some years with amazing, skilful success.

Warsaw, October 1939. German victory parade.

Germany, 1939, showing acquisitions by Hitler up to the outbreak of World War II.

Hitler in Paris, 1940.

The course of World War II is known to all. For the first two and a half years the German armed forces were always victorious on land and usually in the air, while the U-boats were a very real menace beneath the high seas. Poland, Denmark, Norway, Holland, Belgium, France, Yugoslavia, Greece and until December 1941 Russia, it was one long triumph. By then all Europe, from Moscow to Calais, was under German control with only four continental countries, Sweden, Switzerland, Spain and Portugal, cautiously neutral.

The only major rebuff Hitler received was the failure of his air force to conquer Britain, either in battle with the Royal Air Force to open an invasion route for the German army in the summer of 1940 or through the terrorization of the population by indiscriminate bombing of British cities in the winter that followed. Frustrated in the West, in the summer of 1941 Hitler turned upon his loyal and natural ally, Joseph Stalin, and sent into Russia what was probably the finest army, the best led, best equipped and by now highly experienced, that the world had seen since the days of Napoleon. Had the highest German political leaders allowed the generals full control of military operations, it seems probable that Moscow would have fallen, the

The German Army on parade in the Champs-Elysées, during the occupation of Paris.

Russian troops in Stalingrad, 1942.

German transport bogged down in Russian snow.

Red Army thrown back in total disarray to the Urals, and the war in the East would have been another great victory. However just as Hitler's sadism had distracted his air force from its true strategic mission – the destruction of the R.A.F. in the summer of 1940 – in favour of the massacre of civilians, so in 1941 his lust for Ukrainian corn split his army's main effort and delayed it until Russia's greatest ally, snow, ice and sub-zero blizzards, could intervene. This folly was compounded by Hitler's declaration of war on the United States of America in that same December of 1941. With Britain intact, the Red Army battered but unbowed, and America rapidly arming, time was no longer on the side of the Germans. Only a swift victory in the East and in Africa offered the prospect of a favourable outcome.

Both were attempted, at first with success, in 1942 but both failed in the autumn and winter of that year, with the destruction of the Sixth Army at Stalingrad and of *Panzerarmee Afrika* by the British, soon joined by the Americans. Germany attempted one more major offensive on the Eastern Front in the summer of 1943, and this was a complete failure. From then on Germany was on the defensive, almost always, until the end, and Germany's armed forces were slowly driven back in the South, East and finally in the West, fighting with great bravery and skill and suffering appalling casualties both in battle and in the cities which were systematically pulverized by the bombers of the R.A.F. and of the U.S.A.A.F. The young manhood of Germany was more or less wiped out either in battle or in the Russian prisoner-of-war camps, from which few returned. To replace them at the factory benches and on the farms slave labour was employed on a massive scale, the slaves being drawn from the vastly extended concentration-camp system and from the prisoner-of-war camps, or even directly from the occupied territories. Indeed many foreigners were induced or compelled to serve in the German army, usually in a fortress or non-combatant capacity. By the end of the war racial policy had been so far forgotten that one man in every fourteen wearing a German uniform was not a German at all.

Hanover, severely damaged by bombing, 1945, and, *left*, oil refinery attacked by
U.S. Army 8th Air Force, June 1944.

In one field, however, racialism was not forgotten. In 1941 Hitler decided that the time was ripe to destroy physically the entire Jewish population of Europe. How many persons were killed during this 'Final Solution' is open to dispute, the figures varying between three and six millions. No matter what the actual figure was, it branded the Nazi Party and indeed, in the eyes of most of its enemies, Germany as such, as the perpetrators of one of the foulest mass crimes in all history. When at long last the Germans surrendered in May 1945, it was to enemies who hated and despised them and who were determined to punish them for their awful betrayals of civilization and its values. This resulted in the famous Nuremberg Trial of the captured Nazi leaders, most of whom were executed, in many other trials in the course of which less prominent Nazis were sentenced, and in an attempt, which failed, to 'denazify' the entire German nation by the expulsion from public life of all former Nazis. Since almost the entire population had co-operated in some measure or another with the Nazi criminals, it was impossible to find enough 'good' Germans even to carry out the orders of the Occupying Powers.

One ray of decency and hope had shone through elements of the German General Staff and the survivors of the Social Democrat Party who, aware of the crimes that were being committed and later of the fact that Germany could not win the war, attempted to overthrow the government by the assassination of Hitler. They finally failed in July 1944, and several thousand members of this conspiracy were executed. The men who should have run post-Nazi Germany were dead.

Paradoxically, it was once again the Russians who came to Germany's rescue, as after 1918 though now in a very different way. In a deal carried out at Yalta in early 1945 between Stalin, Roosevelt and a somewhat reluctant Winston Churchill, Russia was given a free hand in Eastern Europe and occupation zones were set for a still unoccupied Germany against a future peace treaty with her which had, in fact, never been negotiated, let alone signed. These arrangements gave the Russians all Eastern Germany, with Berlin – to be administered by the four principal Allied Powers, the U.S., Britain, Russia and France jointly – imbedded deep in the heart of the Soviet zone. This partition had endured until the time of writing (1972).

With the departure of the American armed forces imminent and publicly announced, with Britain and France more or less bankrupt, and after the consolidation of Russian power in Eastern Europe, marked by the rape of Czechoslovakia, the Soviets decided in 1948 that it was time to exploit their position of strength. They proceeded, first, to blockade Berlin, their obvious next objective being the American, French and British zones, with the ultimate aim of

Hermann Goering at the Nuremberg
Trial. Condemned to death, he
committed suicide on 15 October
1946.

controlling all Europe. They believed that the Americans who had
handed over Eastern Europe without demur, would give them the
rest of the Continent as well, despite America's monopoly of the
atomic bomb at that time. They were, however, now dealing with a
Truman and not a Roosevelt administration. A massive Anglo-
American airlift kept Berlin alive and free: a massive influx of
American capital allowed Western Europe, including West Germany,
to recover from its post-war penury with astonishing speed: the three
Western-occupied zones were joined into one, further strengthened
economically in the same year by a drastic currency reform: the
Russians lifted their blockade of Berlin, but the American army
remained on West German soil: and in 1949, with the so-called
'economic miracle' well under way, the Western Allies granted a
measure of sovereignty, soon to be almost absolute, to 'their' Germans.
The German Federal Republic was the first child to be born of the
Cold War, a remarkably sturdy infant in view of the circumstances
that prevailed in 1949. The Russians decided to rename their zone the
German Democratic Republic. Austria, soon to be neutralized, had
been created anew. Germany, in fact, was divided as it had not been
for a century. The Germanies existed once again.

Germany today – East and West.

CHAPTER TWELVE

Germany since 1945

The qualities of the German Federal Republic were almost as clearly stamped with the character of Konrad Adenauer as had Nazi Germany been by Hitler or Imperial Germany initially by Bismarck and later by Kaiser Wilhelm II. Adenauer (1876–1967) was a devout Catholic, a non-Nazi but never an active anti-Nazi, a deter-mined anti-Communist and an advocate of the capitalist free-enterprise system. The Nazis had dismissed him as Mayor of Cologne in 1933. In 1945 the British reappointed him, but soon dismissed him in their turn. This did not do him any harm either, in the eyes of the German electorate. He was a proven patriot but not a nationalist, and from the first post-war elections of August 1949 for the next two decades his party, the Christian Democrats, was the largest in the new *Bundes-tag* or Federal Parliament, and Adenauer was chancellor until, in advanced old age but with all his faculties intact, he at last retired in 1963. Though seldom enjoying an absolute majority, the Christian Democrats were able, in coalition with various other right-wing or centre parties, to rule Germany during a long and vital period which saw a transformation from total defeat to extreme prosperity and very considerable strength. The main opposition party, the Social Demo-crats headed by Kurt Schumacher and, after the death of that bitter survival of Weimar, by Willy Brandt, an anti-Nazi who as mayor of Berlin had forcefully and courageously resisted Russian plans of aggression against the city, was equally anti-Communist in its ideology, though more prepared to negotiate with Eastern Europe when at last it took office after the elections of 1969. Somewhat to the surprise of Western liberals, there was no significant revival of any neo-Nazi party in the German Federal Republic. Nor, when it came into existence in the 1950s, did the new German army aspire to the position that its predecessor had held during the Weimar period. It

WIR KÖNNEN NICHT ZAUBERN

1945

ABER ARBEITEN

1949

HILF MIT! WÄHL CDU

ES GEHT UM DEUTSCHLAND!

Christian Democratic Union
election poster, 1949. 'We can't work
miracles, but we can work'.

was loyal to the democratic concepts that lay behind the defensive
alliance called the North Atlantic Treaty Organization. When
General de Gaulle withdrew French forces from N.A.T.O. in the
1960s, the German army became its largest component and, apart
from nuclear weapons, its strongest. Some old soldiers viewed with
disquiet the 'democratic' nature of the new *Bundeswehr*, in which
soldiers can complain of their N.C.O.s and officers to their elected
deputies in the *Bundestag*. However, the new German army and air
force, and the minuscule navy too, appear to be efficient, and certainly
have posed no threat of militarism. The general transition to demo-

Es geht ums Ganze

CDU

'It's a question of the whole'.
C.D.U. poster, 1961.

cracy, in large measure thanks to Adenauer but also due to the temper of post-war Germans, was smooth, easy and – so far as such things can be – comparatively complete.

There were three major issues involved: the economy, the national status, and the reunification of Germany.

To deal with the last issue first, reunification has always been the avowed policy of all German political parties, but the immediate questions that arose were how? and what? The German population had been driven out of East Prussia, of western Poland, of the Sudeten-land, and indeed of parts of East Germany itself. The eastern frontier of

the Communist German Democratic Republic was in effect the Oder-Neisse line, though since there was no peace treaty this has never been formally recognized either by the Bonn government, which 'temporarily' and uncomfortably housed itself within that university town since Berlin was too dangerous and remote, or by the Western Allies. Only reconquest could wrest former German lands from Russians, Poles and Czechs, and West Germany did not and does not have either the means or the temperament for such an adventure. Reunion of two German states then, the Democratic and the Federal Republics? This was always possible, on Russian terms, by the creation of an all-German Soviet state, a solution as unacceptable to the overwhelming majority of West Germans as it was to their great protector, the United States of America. Almost all Germans, east or west of the interzonal border, hated Communism. Indeed Germans from the Russian zone poured into the Federal Republic to such an extent that the Russians and their German Communist satellites were forced to close the border and finally to build a wall straight through Berlin in September 1961. Again there could be no reunification without a war for which neither the Americans nor the Germans were prepared, though both were ready to fight in defence of the territory of the German Federal Republic. As for German-Austria, the *Anschluss* of 1938–45 was not a happy memory, and this issue was never seriously raised again. Thus reunification remained and remains a political slogan and nothing more. Further, in a quarter of a century the two major German states have grown apart. It is probable that responsible men in the Federal Republic would have grave misgivings if the communized inhabitants of the Democratic Republic were suddenly thrust upon them. The age-old concept of 'the Germanies' has prevailed.

Sheltered by the umbrella of American military, and above all nuclear, power, the West Germans were in a position to forget international politics and to concentrate on the economic problems that beset their ruined country, helped in this by a massive influx of American capital with which the name of General George Marshall, then Truman's secretary of state, will always be connected. After World War I, during America's headlong retreat into isolationism, President Calvin Coolidge had remarked that the business of America was business. This point of view exactly suited the Germans of the 1950s. Just as the German governing class had attempted to imitate the French in the eighteenth century and the British in the nineteenth, so now did they copy as best they could the most powerful state of the twentieth. Germany went American, often even thought American, and the result was the so-called 'economic miracle'.

It was an astonishing achievement, though it must be pointed out that its 'miraculous' qualities have been somewhat overstressed. When

The Berlin Wall at the Brandenburg Gate, built by the East German Government in 1961 to halt mass flights of refugees to the West (*left*).

Poster on the Marshall Plan,
issued *c.* 1948.

a country is bankrupt, in ruins and universally abhorred for past crimes and follies that have brought it to such a pass, even a return to normality of wealth and status, in so short a time, must appear a sort of miracle. Furthermore, quite apart from their own industrious nature, Adenauer's Germans had a number of factors working for them in addition to the injection of American capital. In the early days at least they had almost no armed forces to support, their defence being taken care of by their conquerors. The Civil Service, too, that endless drain of wealth and talent in most states, had been so thoroughly purged of Nazis that its numbers were drastically reduced. Hitler had wished to leave Germany a 'scorched earth', and had done his best. The Allies had done theirs, by bombing and later by massive dismantling and confiscation of plant. This meant that German industry had to be, and was, retooled with almost entirely modern equipment in the factories and workshops. Finally the vast influx of German refugees from the East, usually penniless and anxious to find work, meant that German industry had a great pool of skilled and semi-skilled workers upon which to draw, and little need to fear such obstructive trade unionists as were hindering reconstruction in France and Britain: and none of these were Communist saboteurs, in Germany. Soon enough the vast pool of the unemployed was drained, and German industry needed a great many immigrant workers. These came from all over Europe, Greece, Italy, Spain, Turkey, but unlike in Hitler's day they came of their own free will. At the time of writing the German economy is probably the strongest in the world, the *Deutschmark* a harder currency than the dollar.

Man, however, cannot live by hard currency alone and the Germans, perhaps more than other Europeans, have always yearned for an ideal, for a grand design. Old-fashioned, patriotic nationalism had brought them to disaster in two world wars and was thoroughly discredited, particularly among the young who tended to pacifism and an 'include me out' attitude towards the Cold War. Besides, the impossibility of reunification made a nonsense of nationalism. The United Nations, from which the Federal Government was for many years excluded, had at first offered a supra-national ideal, but the Russian abuse of their veto in the Security Council, and the lengthy exclusion of China, combined with the ineffectiveness of the United Nations in the Israeli-Arab and Indo-Pakistani wars, among other failures, deprived it of the status to which it had aspired; politically, at least so far as the Great Powers were concerned, it became little more than a forum in which the issues of the Cold War were debated with acrimony and mistrust. Therefore, to escape not only from the constriction of their new frontiers but also from their own immediate past, the Germans became passionate pan-Europeans.

The Volkswagen factory in Wolfsburg, *above*, and *below*, the Thyssen steel works in Duisburg, the Ruhr.

The first step towards a United Europe was the Schumann plan of 1950 whereby the iron and coal industries of the Six (France, Germany, Italy and the three smaller Benelux countries) were merged in the European Coal and Steel Community. This process was carried further in the years that followed, and in 1957 the Six signed the Treaty of Rome, thus establishing formally the European Economic Community. However the process, even in the economic fields, was a slow one, though immediately and immensely profitable to the countries concerned, and at the time of writing is not fully completed, the unification of agricultural policies having proved among the most intractable problems. Nor has the vast economic expansion of its first decade maintained the original momentum.

Political development of the European Common Market met two formidable obstacles. In the early days the British, who had really sponsored the whole idea, showed no wish to join the Community, principally because they were enmeshed in old imperial dreams – though the Empire had become the Commonwealth – and because of the 'special relationship' with the United States. This and Common-wealth preference in trade were the cornerstones of British policy, and

At a meeting of the German Federal Council, 1963, Willy Brandt, Mayor of Berlin, and Chancellor Adenauer (*right*), speak in favour of close co-operation with France.

The house in which this German farmer's family live was built under a rural development programme.

both must be imperilled by entry into the E.E.C. By the time the British government had changed its mind, in the early 1960s, and applied for membership, General de Gaulle had resumed power in France. He had no wish to see English (or, as he put it, Anglo-American) influence more powerful than it already was in Europe. Indeed he was against the concept of an eventual United States of Europe, preferring his own vision of 'l'Europe des patries', stretching as he rather euphemistically put it from 'the Atlantic to the Urals', for French sovereignty was to him sacrosanct. It is a curious coincidence again that just as nascent French patriotism had put an end to Charlemagne's pan-European or neo-Roman dreams in 843, so de Gaulle's renascent French patriotism eleven centuries later once again destroyed a similar ideal in modern dress. This French withdrawal in the political field was a sad blow to that section, the most admirable, of the

Open-air café in Düsseldorf.

youth of West Germany who had no wish to be forced back into national policies. The German government, on the other hand, had no choice but to accede to this new definition of Europe. The first overt result was a unilateral revaluation of the German currency in 1970. This caused a measure of economic chaos in the whole Western world, scarcely resolved at the time of writing. The second was the opening of straight political negotiations between the West German government, the puppet East German government, and finally the Soviets themselves, in 1971. For his 'new' *Ostpolitik*, which seems to some to foreshadow a return in far more dangerous circumstances to that of the Weimar governments, the West German chancellor, Willy Brandt, was, rather oddly, awarded the Nobel Peace Prize in 1971, denied to the British prime minister, Neville Chamberlain, when he brought back 'peace in our time' from Munich in 1938. The

Lenin Square, East Berlin.
Monument to Lenin erected 1970.

new *Ostpolitik* has certainly further postponed, if it has not actually destroyed, the idea of European political union. Now the British are about to enter the E.E.C. after all, but its political charisma has gone for ever. It is little more than an elaborate trading arrangement.

The alacrity with which the Soviets promulgated a treaty embodying Brandt's *Ostpolitik*: Britain's admission into the E.E.C. in 1973: the probability that the American army will soon depart: and the high level of prosperity in the E.E.C. as a whole and particularly in Germany, all these facts are producing or have produced a Europe with a greater stability than any we have seen in this century. Since more than with most continental countries Germany's fluctuating geography is the root cause of Germany's history, the real acceptance of the present frontiers within the larger E.E.C., combined with the new wealth there, has produced a great measure of tranquillity. Not all Germans, however, were happy with Brandt's *Ostpolitik*.

Some would speak of youthful boredom. Germany's rebuilt cities are, on the whole, unattractive places. There has been no great artistic

Rudi Dutschke, the professional
student agitator, Berlin, 1968.

or literary revival, even such a morbid one as occurred during the
Weimar period. There are no great issues to be debated, no great
ideals to be pursued. And there are indications that the youngest
generation (those born since the creation of the Federal Republic and
usually described as 'students') are in fact reverting to type and casting
about in search of a cause. The materialism of their parents bores them,
as well it might, and many are even flirting with variants of Communism, no doubt largely to annoy their fathers, for no 'student' who
has read anything can fail to see how totally discredited the Marxist
schematic has become, from the Atlantic to the Urals.

On the nature of the next cause that the Germans espouse – assuming
that we are all spared a Third and Ultimate World War – the future
of Germany, and with it of all Europe, will surely depend. But perhaps, with luck, they will not find one at all. If so, this will mean that
at long last they have emerged from political immaturity and assumed
the responsibility and common sense to which every great nation
should aspire.

Chancellor Willy Brandt kneeling in front of the Jewish Heroes' Monument, Warsaw, 7 December 1970.

BIBLIOGRAPHICAL NOTE

Most of the volumes in this series contain a bibliography, one exception being *A Concise History of France*. The reason for this exception is obvious, as I hope is a similar omission from this volume. So much has been written about these two great countries that any bibliography worthy of the name must vastly exceed in length any concise history. Furthermore many aspects of these countries' histories are still open, if not perhaps so much to 'factual argumenta- tion' – at least in modern times (though that exists too) – as to political, intellectual, artistic and even spiritual interpretation. This is perhaps even more true of Germany than of France, though a bibliography of the French Revolution or the Third Republic, of Napoleon or of Louis XIV, would be indeed a formidable task: no less would a bibliography of Martin Luther.

In *A Concise History of Germany* the problem is in many ways even more acute, firstly, owing to the repeated fragmentation of its land and its people and, secondly, owing to the violent ideological oscillations which have re- curred, regardless almost of geography, from the Thirty Years War until the present time. A bibliography of Nazism alone must run to several volumes, though fortunately most of the printed material is easily available in the Wiener Library (London) or in the Institut für Zeitgeschichte (Munich). Indeed a true bibliography, to be of any real value, must include all serious German literature (and who is to decide what is serious and what is not?) as well as all serious criticism, contemporary and posthumous, of that literature. And much the same is true, at least in modern times, of the sciences, both pure and applied, of military theory and practice, of theology, both Roman Catholic and Protestant, of works concerning the plastic arts, economics and industrial development, of the philosophies and their interpretation, both at the time and later, and much of all this written in numerous languages. So, all or nothing. All is obviously an impossibility, a life's work for an academy of scholars engaged upon nothing else. 'Nothing' is, on the other hand, hardly more satisfactory. I do not propose to burden the reader with a list of all the books that I have read on the subject of Germany, a few bucketfuls drawn from an ocean of prose. I would, however, draw his attention to two, neither of which is written for the specialist. One is *A History of Germany* by Robert-Hermann Tenbrock, published in English by the Max Hueber Verlag, Munich, 1968. A cool, rather dry book, written almost entirely from German sources, it gives a panoramic view of German history in a mere 319 pages. It would provide a first-class introduction to this complex subject for graduate or post-graduate students, but it also, alas, has no bibliography. Of far greater literary value and philosophical depth is *The History of Germany since 1789* by Professor Golo Mann, the son of the great novelist. Published originally in 1966, the English edition (Chatto and Windus, London) appeared in 1968. This book does contain a most excellent bibliography, but as its title implies only covers in detail a portion of Germany's history, though to the majority of readers these may be the two most important centuries.

LIST OF ILLUSTRATIONS

34 Louis IV of Bavaria endowing Dietrich von Altenburg, Grand Master of the Teutonic Order with Lithuanian lands, 1337. Staatsarchiv Königsberg, Schriebl. 20 Nr. 29. Göttingen.

34 Henry IV imploring Matilda of Tuscany and Abbot Hugh of Cluny to intercede for him with Pope Gregory VII. Early twelfth-century MS. Biblioteca Apostolica Vaticana.

35 Frederick Barbarossa with his sons Henry VI and Frederick of Swabia. History of the Welfs of Weingarten, c. 1180. *Fulda* MS. Hessische Landesbibliothek.

36 Tannhäuser, dressed as a Teutonic knight. *Minnesinger* MS, c. 1300. Universitäts-Bibliothek, Heidelberg.

38 Map of Acre. MS from *Historia Anglorum* by Matthew Paris, before 1259. British Museum.

39 Marienburg Castle, seat of the Grand Master of the Teutonic Order from 1309. *Photo Deutscher Kunstverlag, Bavaria.*

40 Teutonic Knights Quarters, Nuremberg. Diagrammatic plan by Hans Bien, 1625. Germanisches Nationalmuseum, Nuremberg.

41 Town church, Wittenberg. Woodcut from *Wittenberger Heiligthumsbuch* by Lucas Cranach the Elder, 1509. Öffentliche Kunstsammlung, Basel.

42 Martin Luther. Painting by Lucas Cranach the Elder, c. 1525. Öffentliche Kunstsammlung, Basel.

42 The three Saxon Electors: left to right, Frederick the Wise, John the Steadfast and John Frederick. Paintings by Lucas Cranach the Elder. Kunsthalle, Hamburg.

43 Emperor Charles V. Painting by Christoph Amberger (1500–61). Staatliche Museen, Berlin. *Photo Marburg.*

44 Title-page of pamphlet by Luther, c. 1520. British Museum. *Photo John Freeman.*

45 'The Peasants' Army'. Title-page of pamphlet issued in 1525. British Museum. *Photo John Freeman.*

45 Ulrich von Hutten. Woodcut portrait by Erhard Schoen, c. 1520. Kupferstich Kabinett, Berlin. *Photo Walter Steinkopf.*

47 'Beast of War'. Broadsheet, published during Thirty Years War. Stadtarchiv, Ulm.

47 Siege of Münster, 1534–35. Engraving by H. Sebald Beham. British Museum. *Photo John Freeman.*

48 Ratification of Treaty of Münster, 15 May 1648. Painting by Gerard Ter Borch (1617–81). National Gallery, London.

49 Battle of Blenheim, 1704. Engraving by Jan van Huchtenberg, 1720. British Museum. *Photo John Freeman. George Rainbird Archives.*

50 Map of Germany during the early seventeenth century.

52 Hohenzollern Castle. Engraving from *Merian's Topography*, 1646–53, facsimile 1959. British Museum. *Photo Eileen Tweedy.*

53 Berlin, the royal palace. Engraving by J. Rosenberg, 1781. British Museum. *Photo John Freeman.*

54 Coronation of Frederick I of Prussia. Engraving from *Die Königliche Preussische Crönung*, 1712. British Museum. *Photo John Freeman.*

54 *Tabakscollegium* of Frederick I of Prussia in the Berlin royal palace, 1710. Painting by P. C. Leygebe. Neues Palais, Potsdam. *Photo Staatliche Schlösser und Gärten, Potsdam.*

55 Frederick the Great, as a boy, dressed in uniform of a grenadier. Painting, Eremitage, Bayreuth. *Photo Staatsbibliothek, Berlin.*

56 Sans-Souci Palace, Potsdam. Designed by W. von Knobelsdorff, 1745–47. *Photo Marburg.*

56 Frederick the Great visiting territories at Rhinluch. Painting by G. von Frisch (1730–1815). Schloss Charlottenburg. *Photo Staatsbibliothek, Berlin.*

57 Frederick the Great visiting Voltaire. Engraving by Pierre-Charles Baquoy after painting by Nicolas André Monsiaux (1754–1837). Staatsbibliothek, Berlin.

57 Frederick the Great returning from manœuvres. Painting by E.F. Cunningham. Sans-Souci, Potsdam. *Photo Staatliche Schlösser und Garten.*

58 Johann Wolfgang von Goethe (1749–1832). Painting by J.E. Schumann, after G.M. Kraus, 1778. Goethe Museum, Frankfurt. *Photo Freies Deutsches Hochstift.*

58 Friedrich von Schiller (1759–1805). Painting by Anton Graff, 1791. Museum für Stadtgeschichte, Dresden. *Fotothek Dresden.*

58 Gotthold Ephraim Lessing (1729–81). Painting by Anton Graff. *Photo Marburg.*

59 Johann Gottfried Herder (1744–1803). Painting after Fr Rehberg, c. 1787. Nationale Forschungs- und Gedenkstätten in Weimar.

59 Gottfried Wilhelm Leibniz (1646–1716). After painting by A. Scheits. *Photo Staatsbibliothek, Berlin.*

59 Immanuel Kant, aged forty-four. Woodcut by A. Neumann after painting by I. B. Becker. *Photo Staatsbibliothek, Berlin.*

60 Students at Jena University. Anonymous eighteenth-century watercolour. Galerie Fischer, Lucerne.

61 University Library, Göttingen. Engraving by G. D. Heumann. Germanisches National-museum, Nuremberg.

62 Johann Sebastian Bach, aged thirty-five. Painting by Johann Jakob Ihle. *Photo Staatsbibliothek, Berlin.*

63 Pilgrimage church of Vierzehn-heiligen, Main Valley. Designed by Johann Balthasar Neumann (1743–72). *Photo Hirmer Photoarchiv.*

64 Columbine and Brighella. Porcelain group by J. J. Kändler, Meissen factory, mid-eighteenth century. Victoria and Albert Museum, London.

66 Castle and garden of Pommers-felden. Engraving by Salomon Kleiner (1703–61). *Photo Marburg.*

66 Friedrich Hölderlin (1770–1843). Pastel portrait by F. K. Hiemer. *Photo Staatsbibliothek, Berlin.*

67 N. Copernicus (1473–1543). After a woodcut by Tobias Stimmer, *c.* 1587. Deutsches Museum, Munich.

67 Statue of Roland, 1404. Market square, Bremen. *Photo Presse und Informationsamt, Bonn.*

68 Feudal scene depicting a whip-ping. Engraving, end of eighteenth century. *Photo Archiv Gerstenberg.*

69 Capture of Regensburg, 1809. Painting by Charles Thevenin. Musée de Versailles. *Photo Service de Documentation Photographique.*

70 The Princes of the Confedera-tion of the Rhine acclaim Napo-leon as their protector, 1806. Contemporary lithograph. *Photo Archiv Gerstenberg.*

70 Napoleon receiving the deputies of the Senate in the royal palace in Berlin, November 1806. Painting by René-Theodore Berthon, 1808. Musée de Ver-sailles. *Photo Hachette.*

71 Return of the Elector of Hesse from exile, 1813. Contem-porary engraving. *Germanisches Nationalmuseum, Nuremberg.*

72 Napoleon and Marie Louise arriving at the Tuileries, 1810. Musée de Versailles. Painting. *Photo Service de Documentation Photographique.*

73 Battle of the Nations at Leipzig, October 1813. Contemporary engraving. *Photo Staatsbibliothek, Berlin.*

74 Map of Germany in 1815 by Claus Henning.

75 The artist's family. Coloured drawing by Friedrich Wilhelm Doppelmayr, 1831. German-isches Nationalmuseum, Nuremberg.

76 Karl Marx (1818–83). *Photo International Instituut voor Social Geschiedenis, Amsterdam.*

76 Krupp Steel Works in 1819. Contemporary engraving. *Photo F. Krupp, Essen.*

77 Germany after an imaginary suspension of the Customs Union. Cartoon, *Kladderadatsch,* 1852. *Photo Eileen Tweedy.*

79 Watch on the Rhine. German cartoon, *c.* 1840. Thames and Hudson Archives.

80 Hall of Fame, with statue of 'Bavaria', Munich. Designed by Leo von Klenze, 1843–50. *Photo Marburg.*

81 Castle Falkenstein. Design by Christian Jank, 1883. *Photo W. Neumeister.*

81 Tannhäuser on the Venusberg. Mural by J. Aigner, 1881. Neuschwanstein. *Photo W. Neumeister.*

83 'To my dear Berliners.' Con-temporary lithograph. Mär-kisches Museum, Berlin.

84 The Frankfurt Assembly in the St Paulskirche, 1848. *Leipziger Illustrierte Zeitung.* British Mu-seum. *Photo John Freeman.*

86 Map of Germany 1871–1914 by Claus Henning.

88 Prince Metternich. Painting by Thomas Lawrence, 1819. Bun-deskanzleramt, Vienna. *Photo Österreichische Nationalbibliothek.*

89 Otto von Bismarck-Schönhau-sen, deputy to the Landtag, 1847. Engraving after a family portrait. *Mansell Collection.*

90 Nursery, attached to factory, 1880s. *Leipziger Illustrierte Zei-tung. Photo Eileen Tweedy.*

90 German Social Insurance, 1913. Contemporary illustra-tion. *S.P.D. Archiv, Bonn.*

91 Krupp's Great Cannon at the Paris International Exhibition, 1867. *Leipziger Illustrierte Zei-tung. Photo Eileen Tweedy.*

93 Council of War, 1870. Painting by Anton von Werner (1843–1915). *Photo Staatliche Museen, Berlin.*

INDEX

References to illustrations are printed in italics